CW00518388

NOT QUITE THE END

A Journey Through End Stage Renal Disease

UMMU AHMADAIN

PARTRIDGE

Library of Congress Control Number: 2021910837
ISBN: Hardcover   978-1-5437-6511-3
               Softcover   978-1-5437-6510-6
               eBook   978-1-5437-6512-0

Print information available on the last page.

To order additional copies of this book, contact
Toll Free +65 3165 7531 (Singapore)
Toll Free +60 3 3099 4412 (Malaysia)
orders.singapore@partridgepublishing.com

www.partridgepublishing.com/singapore

*This revised edition of this book is dedicated
with love and gratitude to:
My beloved sister, Oni, her husband, Along, and
their lovely daughters, Emma, Inaz, and Olin,
for giving me a second chance in life*

*Zul, Ashraf, and Zakiy for making my life complete and
Adzkia and Nasreen for making my boys' lives complete*

Aya and Yahya, the apples of my eyes

*Abah, Mak, Ba', and Mok, may Allah bless their souls,
my brothers and sisters for all their support*

*All the hospital staff who helped make my life that
bit more bearable during those trying times*

*My fellow ESRD friends who have showed me
the meaning of patience and acceptance,
wherever they may be.*

CONTENTS

AUTHOR'S NOTE

Ordinary! That is how I would describe myself. I would certainly be lost in oblivion amid even twenty people—just a plain individual with an ordinary life.

And that's why I wonder why it happened to me.

Certainly, it was a test for me from God. Or perhaps some would say it was a punishment from God for some sins I may have committed. But I prefer to hold on to the former. I believe in a God who is most beneficent and most compassionate. And He has created me, as with all other creatures, to test who among His creations acknowledge His presence and greatness. Perhaps I needed a stronger nudge to be reminded of Him. Better yet, I would like to believe the stronger nudge was to give me a chance to move a notch closer to Him. God knows that, for some of His servants, it is difficult and not enough for them to do good deeds. And so, God will send them trials in the form of sickness, amongst others to build their characters and bring them closer to Him.

Today, I do believe there's some truth in the phrase, "What does not kill you makes you stronger." And I believe strongly, too, that everything that happens to us happens with a purpose. There are no coincidences in life—everything is with a purpose. Perhaps it was never about me after all. Perhaps all the trials I went through were a preparation for me to be an instrument of something greater. What I went through all those years of my illness has indeed left me with a better and a humbler view of what life means, at least to me; and maybe that is what I needed to raise my children and make them outstanding individuals in their times, God willing.

Or it could be that my experience is destined to affect another unsuspecting individual—someone I may have never met or will never know. What happened to me happened a long time ago. But by the grace of God, it remains fresh in my memories. At times, I wish I could forget the things that happened then. But more often than not, they constantly remind me to hang on when life sucks, to grit my teeth when I feel like giving up, and to always thank God when I am so full of myself. Recalling all this on paper will be my legacy to my children, and hopefully, it can be a beacon to someone who's about to give up hope, to someone who is about to surrender before giving out a fight, or to a lost soul who cannot see the wisdom in God's strange ways. I don't really know.

What I do know is this—it is my staunch belief that, even if there's only one person who benefits from this effort of mine, I have fulfilled at least one tiny responsibility to God and humankind.

What's meant to be will always find its way.

CHAPTER

1

The Start of the End

ESRD! That was the start of things. End-stage renal disease—or simply kidney failure (today it's called end-stage kidney disease). I was just living my ordinary life when it chose to come into my life and make significant to me all that was to follow. It came at a time when I was working hard to make something of my life. I was in my final year of university studying biology with the hope that, when I graduated, my life would change, and I would go on to make my mark in life. Nothing was supposed to stand in the way of my obtaining my honours degree, until one fateful day when my best friend Habibah shocked me back into a grim reality.

"Fizah, really you shouldn't. How many have you taken today already?"

Habibah shook her head as she watched me gulp down my twelfth tablet of paracetamol with a glass of cold water. Those were the words that started my whirlwind rendezvous with ESRD.

This I have learnt: Blessed is the person with friends who genuinely care for her and who are sensitive enough to notice changes in her.

Habibah and I were very close. Yet we were as opposite as any two individuals could be. She was very fair and Chinese looking, quiet and fairly calm. I was slim and dark and definitely more mischievous. We came from the same hometown but only met each other when we were both selected to the same boarding school, in the capital city of Kuala Lumpur, at thirteen. We were placed in the same dormitory, and our friendship grew stronger and closer over the span of the nearly six years we were there. There were not many secrets that we did not share. Then, at eighteen, both of us were sent to Grantham College for further education in England on a scholarship. Later it was just assumed that we would apply to the same university too. She became like a sister, as well as a best friend. We truly watched each other's back, and whatever did not seem right between us, we voiced.

Over the years, Habibah (now Datuk Dr Habibah), with her thick glasses, became one friend who truly knew my ups and downs and could tolerate all my irksome moods. She was the cool one. I could be quite deviant at times. But both of us knew without saying that our studies were the uppermost priority when we were in the United Kingdom.

It was because of this that she was quick to notice how I'd missed class several times and how, whenever she saw me, I would be shoving some painkiller down my throat. What she did not know was all the headaches I was suffering from at that time. My head would feel as if it was being squeezed on both sides; at other times, it felt as if a giant chain ball was trashing it. No part of my head was spared of this unbearable pain. The headaches were simply too strong and were severely preventing me from doing anything else. The finals were just round the corner. I needed to stay alert and focused. At times, it was all I could do to get up and perform the five daily prayers. Yet I had to pass the finals. After five years in England, so far away from the people I loved, I had to make my stay worthwhile.

"It's okay, Habibah; I can handle this. I just need the tablets to perk me up a bit more. Don't worry about me."

"But how many of those pills have you actually taken, Fizah? That's what you said when you were taking eight of them. How many exactly have you taken today?" she repeated the question.

"Twelve," I whispered, feeling like a miscreant schoolgirl caught by the discipline teacher.

"What?" I watched as Habibah gasped. I could see that she was not pleased with my reply.

"I don't care, Fizah. By hook or by crook, tomorrow you will get yourself to the university clinic and get a check-up done. And no arguing."

Although Habibah and I were the same age, and she was normally a mild-natured woman, when she was in that mood, I would do well not to argue with her. God bless her for her persistence.

Still, I tried to present my case. "It must be the grapes I ate over the weekend, Bibs. You know me; I get drunk just from eating grapes. I must be having a hangover right now." I made a feeble attempt to joke about it.

Ironically, the joke was not too far from the truth. I was never much of a fruit person before; and I was very selective of the fruits I ate. Bananas and papayas topped my list of favourite fruits, but while they cost next to nothing back in Malaysia, they cost a fortune in England. So, being a student on scholarship, I usually went for the cheaper, easy-to-eat fruits—the grapes. I never really fancied grapes, because even in my days in Malaysia, whenever I ate grapes, I would start to feel woozy, and my whole body would feel disoriented. It would be as if there was no communication between my body and my head. I never knew why at that time. In England, however, I ate more grapes than I ever did in Malaysia, only to suffer some form of hangover afterwards—up to the point that my housemates would jokingly claim that I did not have to drink alcohol to get drunk; I would already be drunk just from eating the grapes!

(I found out later that it is not advisable for people with my condition to eat grapes—they increase the potassium level in the body, which can affect the heart.)

So, under Habibah's severe stare, it was decided I would be going to the university clinic the next day.

On Monday, as it turned out, I had only one lecture to attend. I was in my final year of study in the field of biology, majoring in physiology and zoology at the University of Salford. As it happened, it was just a fifty-minute lecture at the Chapman Hall. Still, I was too agitated to pay any attention to the zoology lecture. Immediately after class, I headed straight from the then Biology Tower Building to the clinic in the university grounds. I had no wish to trouble either of my two friends who were studying the same course as I was, so I decided to go on my own. After all, the clinic was still on university grounds. As I walked alone under the grey autumn skies, moving briskly, the strong winds were gathering the leaves on the road, which rustled crisply under my feet. There was not much sunshine, and I noticed there were not many students outside. It was just more comfortable to stay indoors.

This was the second time I'd visited the clinic—the first time being a visit to get my rubella shot. It was the university ruling that all female undergraduates take the shot. As I closed the door of the clinic entrance behind me, the warmth of the small room was a most welcome change to the strong winds outside. It was quiet, apart from the slow classical music in the background, and there was a faint smell of floor disinfectant in the air. The whitewashed room took away some of my anxieties as I sat waiting for my name to be called. Looking around, I realised I was the only patient in the clinic, and I knew it would not be too long before I was called to see the doctor. I never liked going to see any doctor or going to hospital for that matter. Hah! Little did I know that, for the next few years, I was to spend more time in a hospital than at home!

When my name was called out, a kindly looking middle-aged female doctor with short greying hair and a white doctor uniform ushered me in. Dr. Tarsh was of medium height and had a smile, which I found quite reassuring as I explained to her about the recurring headaches. She nodded seriously and then raised her brows when I mentioned taking twelve tablets of painkillers almost every day for the past month. Somehow, I was not surprised when she immediately took my blood pressure.

What surprised both of us was that my blood pressure reading was way above the normal blood pressure of 120/80. No wonder I was having those killer headaches. I remember Dr Tarsh looking at me without saying a word for what seemed like a very long time. Her silence brought back my worries and gave me the shivers.

"Any individual below the age of twenty-five should never have this kind of blood pressure reading, and you are just twenty-two, Miss Manaf. That's saying there is something wrong somewhere. I have one main suspicion here," she finished off gravely. Still, she was not letting me in on what was on her mind.

"I want you to take a urine sample, and we will see what it says," she said and buzzed the nurse to give me a urine sample bottle. The nurse led me to the toilet to collect a urine sample for the urine FEME test. It's a basic clinical test to check if there's any protein leak in the urine and how badly. That was to be the first of my numerous urine FEME tests throughout my life; I still have them even today.

Dr Tarsh shook her head at the results that came back. The slip of paper showed a protein count of "++++". I remember my heart beating so rapidly I found it difficult to breathe normally. Although I had no idea what those plusses meant, from the serious look on Dr Tarsh's face, I knew it was not good news she had for me.

"Just as I expected. You see these plusses here? This means that you are leaking protein in your urine, and a lot; you are probably having some kind of renal problem, and that is probably why you are having the high blood pressure and the headaches. Most probably it could be something to do with your kidneys. I want you to do some further tests immediately, so I'm going to arrange a hospital appointment for you, young lady."

Wait a minute!

Problems with my kidneys?

My mind was spinning fast. I had just learnt about the kidneys and osmoregulation in my physiology class. The kidneys filter out the toxic wastes from our body and regulate the ionic balance of our body fluid and, hence, our blood pressure. They have these very tiny structures called nephrons that allow only the smallest of particles to pass through them. Large molecules like proteins and red blood cells are too big and cannot pass through the filter. Therefore, technically I should not find proteins or blood in my urine. This was all due to the millions of these filtering structures that determine what can come out in our urine and what cannot.

I could feel goosebumps spreading all over my body. I had also learnt that these nephrons, once damaged, could never be replaced. When the nephrons of the kidneys are diseased or damaged, there is no repair. It's a degenerative condition. This certainly did not sound good to me. What if the nephrons in my kidneys were damaged?

Everything else became a blur after that. What stands out in my memory today is the barrage of questions that screamed in my head throughout the walk back home to the university flat. Dr Tarsh had explained that depending on the severity of the condition of my kidneys, a worst-case scenario would be either a lifelong dependency on dialysis or a renal transplant. But she also told me not to worry; it could be only a temporary thing I was having at that moment. Still, "dialysis", "renal transplant"—they were big words. What did they mean? My mind was jammed.

Walking briskly, it would normally take about fifteen minutes to get from the university to Poplar Court, the students' accommodation where I lived. I guess I needed the cold air to grasp what the doctor had said and to assess the situation I was in. I hadn't even realised I had walked all the way home, oblivious to the cold wintry noon. It was only as I approached the building that I finally felt the cold winds stinging my nose.

Slowly, everything began to make sense.

It was no wonder I was steadily losing weight, despite my good appetite for food. I had attributed it earlier to being far away from home and missing my family. I had always been a slim person, but when I first came to England, I had put on quite a bit of weight, which, to me at that time felt good. But I soon realised it was only a passing thing. By the time I was in my final year of study, I was never able to get back to that ideal weight of fifty-five kilograms.

But more importantly, the finals were just around the corner.

I can't be having kidney problems—not now, I screamed in my head.

I was in my final year at the university. Passing the final exam was imperative. My parents back home were waiting for me to return with my success.

My parents— what should I tell them? Dr Tarsh had said she strongly suspected that probably both my kidneys were affected, but she could not be sure. That would require further investigations at a hospital. She had mentioned big words for treatment like "renal transplant" and "lifelong dialysis", whatever they meant. I simply had no idea then. So how would I tell my parents I was not well here in England? They would be out of their minds with worry! There was no doubt in my mind they would. My father, a retired teacher, although a strict disciplinarian, was passionate about his feelings, especially where his children were concerned. If he was angry, it would be all hell breaking loose. But if anyone of us was in any trouble or in pain, he could be emotionally moved to tears—a man with very strong emotions indeed. I simply could not have him and my mother losing sleep worrying about me.

Throughout that slow walk back to my flat, I had forgotten I was wearing only my thin grey blazer over my blue cotton *baju kurung*, our national costume. It was only when I reached my flat about twenty minutes later that I felt the biting cold air all over my body. My two housemates, Hanizan, a first-year student and Hafiza, an Algerian doing her master's degree, were not home yet. The house was strangely quiet, and my problem seemed to loom larger in the silence. I climbed upstairs and rushed straight to the toilet.

I have a dark complexion but staring back at me in the bathroom mirror was a pallid face with eyes that were about to burst into tears. The water vapours condensing on the lenses of my spectacles slowly clouded my vision. Leaning against the toilet sink and taking a deep breath to soothe my erratic nerves, I watched as the blood slowly returned to my nose and cheeks with a sting that pinched me back to reality. And as reality started to hit home—slowly and painfully—I gripped the bath sink tightly with both hands just so I would not collapse from the helpless feelings slowly clutching my heart. I was suddenly enshrouded in a dark hopeless cloud of despair and uncertainty.

Much as I tried to downplay my worries, I could not help but think the worst at that time. All I could think of was I had kidney problems—pending total breakdown. My future was no longer certain. All my dreams, my desires, and my ambition were now on hold. It was too much for me to take in, to digest.

And then, out of the blue, I remembered the prayer I was taught to recite every time a calamity befell me or if I heard of one:

From God we come, and unto Him we shall return.

(The Cow [Al Baqarah] 2:156)

I said the prayer out loud.

And then I threw up.

CHAPTER

2

_____

Questions, Questions, Questions

═══════════════════════════════

Sometimes all you can do is not think,
not wonder, not imagine, not obsess. Just
breathe and have faith that everything will work out
for the best.

═══════════════════════════════

With the referral letter from Dr Tarsh, I managed to fix an appointment with the Salford Royal Hospital in Greater Manchester.

It was another cold and wet morning when I took the number 68 bus from the Salford Precinct, just across the street from Poplar Court where I was staying, for my first hospital appointment. Along the way, as the bus weaved into lanes and streets on its way to Manchester's Piccadilly station, my meandering mind wandered and contemplated what I was about to go through once I reached the hospital.

What if it is really kidney failure?

Will I survive it?

Am I going to die?

Prior to this, back in Malaysia, I hardly ever went to hospital. The last time I'd been was when I'd had to do a medical check-up before I left for the United Kingdom. In the past, whenever I was not well, I would just swallow some painkillers and sleep myself off till I got well again—which would only be for about a day or so. I was never ill for a long time. I ate a lot, but I never needed to worry about putting on weight. So my slim build was never a concern to anyone or even to myself. I thought hard.

What could possibly have caused this renal problem?

As the bus went past the university grounds, my anxiety grew. I was clueless as to what was in store for me. In no time I was at the corner of the junction where the red brick hospital building stood, and the bus stopped to let me off. At that time, the hospital was just over a hundred years old, and the historical building looked quite formidable. I felt jittery as my anxiety grew.

Since I had come early to the hospital, I did not have to rush around looking for the outpatient department, and the waiting was not too long either before my number was called out. My heart thumped hard against my chest.

"This way, please." The nurse who'd called my name cheerfully led me to a room where a male doctor was sitting behind a rather cluttered table.

Now, I was not used to talking to male strangers, let alone an English one, and my unease escalated to quite an alarming degree as I sat and watched the thin and scraggly young doctor browse through the referral letter from Dr Tarsh. In between reading, he looked up at me and smiled. But unfortunately, that was not quite enough to appease my tension.

Then he started asking me questions.

It was more like an exhaustive interrogation.

"Back in Malaysia, would you say you live in a town or a village?" he would ask. "Do you have a proper sanitation system at home, or do you have outdoor toilets?" Much to my chagrin, he would ask, "Do you have taps in your house, or does your water supply come from dug out wells? What about electricity? Do you have electricity in your home?"

Such exhaustive questions. He asked questions to the minutest detail about my home and lifestyle back in Malaysia (more of this later). I lived just twenty minutes from town, which was not much different from the conditions here in Salford.

Thereafter followed a general abdominal examination before he informed me that my condition warranted further examination. I watched anxiously as he scribbled something on a form and told me to make an appointment for the test.

It wasn't long before I was back at the hospital for a barium test.

This time around, I was immediately directed through a small yellow brick corridor that led to the imaging room. I handed my appointment letter to the radiologist, a tall English man in a white lab coat who had a friendly smile. I was simply too nervous to smile back at him. He must have noticed my anxiety because he smiled even more and spoke to me quietly and clearly. He explained to me explicitly why and how the procedure was to be carried out.

"Right then. What we are going to do here is that I am going to inject into your vein a certain blue dye, which contains barium actually, and as the dye moves through your veins, you will begin to feel a tingling sensation, especially to both your lips up here and 'down there'."

Then he patted me on the shoulder and said, "Don't worry. It won't hurt at all."

Even in my tension, I had to smile, albeit shakily.

Personally, I was grateful for his explanation. I feel patients should know any procedure that is about to be done unto them. I certainly would want to know. The rationale of knowing what is about to happen to my body can have both a comforting and calming effect. Enlightenment is a blessing actually.

As I reclined onto the stretcher, the steel of the board felt cold under my touch. I could not be sure if it was the metal or my hands that were cold. My heart was pounding as I tried to absorb the rather dark surrounding. All around me suddenly looked cold and menacing. I was not sure what to do next.

"Do I have to take off my headdress?" I asked the radiologist timidly. I was feeling extremely anxious by that time.

"No ... no ... you can keep it on," he replied in a voice that I thought sounded cheerful under the circumstances. "I just need you to roll up your sleeve here," pointing to my left arm.

I suppose the radiologist must have noticed my fear, from my fast and shallow breathing. Gently he touched my arm as he reminded me not to worry once again. "Take it easy. This won't hurt."

The injection was bearable, as with any other venous injections. But as the blue dye moved slowly through my body, I remember feeling being dragged down—a really heavy sensation bearing down on my body. Lying down made breathing even more difficult, and I reckoned it must have been apparent, for the radiologist explained that barium is a metal with a relatively high mass. No wonder I felt pinned down. And then it came—the tingling sensation to my lips that made my mouth felt dry and almost impossible to open—admittedly a most queer experience to me. It was not pain that I felt, just a dull pins-and-needles sensation. The sensation spread to all parts of my body, just like the radiologist had warned me earlier.

The anxiety and the effect of the barium made my breathing more laboured. I had to try to calm myself. And once again, I resorted to the one way I knew how. Closing my eyes, I began to recite the zikr, quietly invoking all the attributes of God. The zikr had never failed to calm and soothe my jittery nerves. It worked every time.

Before I knew it, it was all over.

When it was all done, I thanked the Almighty silently with a big sigh of relief. Little did I know at that time that it was to be a journey of getting close to Him, calling out to Him, seeking strength and patience through Him, and having a personal relationship with my Creator.

It is true, as the saying goes, that often great adversity is truly "a blessing in disguise". I was afflicted with renal problems, but I know now this was certainly the moment when I was most blessed to experience His love and mercy. To the world outside, it would seem as if God was abandoning me, and I was losing out on my youth; but the truth is, the experience brought me closer to Him, and it helped me mature beyond my years. I believe what I got from my illness has made me a more resilient person today.

Following the results of my barium test, I was informed that I needed to go through more tests. For that, I needed to be admitted into the hospital.

A hospital admission? I had never been admitted to a hospital before in my whole life. I had mixed feelings of fear and hope. Why was this happening to me so suddenly? One minute, I had been just living my life quietly as a student, focusing on my finals; and the next minute, I was suddenly a sick girl pending renal failure. Why me? Why then? I was praying hard that all the tests I was about to take would only show that I was fine and that nothing was seriously wrong with me—that it was all just a minor glitch in my health. Yet, at the back of my mind,

I was afraid that the results would show this bad dream was, indeed, real.

What would I do then?

How would I cope?

November 1983

It was around that time that my birthday came and went quietly and uneventfully. The only surprise I got for my birthday was the diagnosis of pending renal failure. There I was— twenty-two years old and about to graduate from university soon. The world was out there for me to grasp; my ambition to become a teacher was about to be realised. A young woman, I had the world was on my doorstep for the taking. All my life, this was what I had worked for.

I was the second youngest of ten other siblings. With four older brothers and five older sisters, I could say I was well protected, cocooned by my family. I grew up pretty much doing my own thing, not really demanding much attention. I have one younger sister, so I wasn't particularly being pampered either. Maybe that made me more of a silent observer than a talker in the house. With so many siblings, when at home, I mingled mostly only with them for most of the time.

When I was ten, I watched as one of my older brothers Zafik went off to a boarding school. It impressed me so much that, by going to a boarding school, he got his own stuff—his own bunk and locker, his own pocket money. Although I lived in a fairly large house, with a huge lounge and dining area, there were eleven of us in the house plus my parents, which made thirteen of us altogether—not to mention the perpetual in and outflow of cousins who were sent to my home for a tour of stay under my father's supervision. My father was a schoolmaster and a strict one at that, so uncles and aunts would send their children with the hope they would turn out to be somebody under my father's disciplined care. You can be sure there was never a moment of privacy in the house.

Imagine then what I felt when I saw my brother with the "luxury" of having his own things. I was determined to get myself into a boarding school and get that much desired privacy. But to get there, I had to excel in my studies. That was what spurred me on, and since then I had braced myself to be the best in my studies at any cost.

I spent my primary days attending the Methodist Girls Primary School not far from home—an English-medium missionary school. My father wanted his children to be well versed in English. I presume, as a teacher himself, he knew the advantages of being able to speak English. My ambition to go off to a boarding school drove me to excel. I must thank God that, as a child, I was blessed with a sharp mind and quick to remember what I was taught. So, excel I did. I was in an all-girls school, so I was rather uninhibited to voice out and be my true self. My constant good results and my assertiveness led me to be the head prefect of the school at that time. There was no stopping me from achieving the best for myself.

And then, when I was 13, my wish did come true. My hard work paid off.

I got an offer to a brand-new fully residential school—the Selangor Science Secondary School in Kuala Lumpur, about an hour's drive from home. I was initially quite surprised that it was a co-ed school. Most of the residential schools I'd known prior to this were either only for boys or only for girls. This was something I was totally unused to. I was never comfortable with boys. The only males I mingled with were my brothers and my father.

Of course, I finally got all my own things. But I later learnt that I was quite deluded about the privacy I'd hoped for. It turned out that I had to share the dormitory with thirteen other girls. And I learnt the hard lesson of missing home and my siblings—and especially my parents. I missed home-cooked food. Being in a co-ed school and unused to having boys as classmates, I missed being my free and vocal self. The situation was not too bad in the dormitory though. But I didn't really enjoy myself overall at the boarding school initially. (I never quite got over my homesickness, even until my senior years actually.) Still, I kept my studies as my core business, and I told myself that, to succeed, something had to give. Sacrifices had to be made.

To me, it was a heavy price to pay indeed. I never knew that missing home and my family could eat away at my heart so torturously. The pangs of missing home were sometimes so overwhelming that, on occasion, I fell physically sick and was down with fever. But each time I fell sick, I just slept it off, not taking any medication for the fever. I kept telling myself that, over time, I would get over it. And eventually, time did dull the pain somewhat.

I was in boarding school for five years. There were more boys than girls in the school at that time. Hailing from an all-girls school, I never did quite manage to adjust to a co-ed environment. I found it rather stressful to have to talk to boys.

Thus, I ended up quite withdrawn in the classroom but more my own self in the dormitory with the girls. Throughout the years, my primary focus was to get to the top, and that proved to be a somewhat challenging task. All the other students had been selected based on their excellent performance at their primary school. They were equally sharp and bright.

The most significant thing that impacted me was, year in and year out, I would watch as my seniors rejoiced from their excellent performances in the national examinations, and one by one, many would leave on scholarship to study overseas—mainly the United Kingdom, the United States of America, and Australia. That soon became my drive for my quest for success. I was determined that, one, day I would join the ranks.

Success became an intense thing for me. It wasn't enough that I was good in my studies; I had to be excellent enough to secure a scholarship to continue my studies overseas.

And along with the intensive drive to excel came the headaches and the stomach upsets.

Still, God must have heard my prayers and granted me my wish. At 18, I was off to the United Kingdom, together with my classmate Habibah, to do A levels at the Grantham College for Further Education in Lincolnshire. Those were among the best years of my life. And when I returned for the summer holidays the following year, I had gained weight considerably and was definitely several tones fairer of skin. But surely the most profound of all was that I finally learnt what it meant for me to be a Muslim, and I began to understand my relationship with God. It is rather ironic really—to have been born and raised in a Muslim country but to discover Islam in a foreign non-Muslim nation.

In Grantham, there were three others who I grew particularly close to, Habibah included. Habibah, Siti, and I were planning to major in biology, and the fourth, Mastura, was going to read physics. We practically went everywhere together. It was a unanimous decision to continue our studies at the University of Salford in Manchester. And that was how Habibah and I ended up in the same university too.

I was determined to graduate and make my parents proud of me. In later years, as a further incentive, the university had given out offers for us foreign students to continue straight into the masters' programme pending good results of the finals. This was like a dream come true—a shortcut to my plans in life.

I had initially planned to teach for a few years and then apply to do my master's and eventually become a lecturer at a university. That was the long-term ambition. I had so many things planned in my head—save some money and travel for vacations, get my driving license, buy a good car and travel across Malaysia and later even overseas perhaps. I also made special plans to focus on my writing—my passion since I was a little girl.

So, I wonder today if my driven self was what triggered the ESRD. Was that why my kidneys failed me? Did they just get too stressed out?

Along the way, marriage was included I suppose, although I never quite gave it any serious thought back then. I had no beauty to boast—I was thin, dark, and bespectacled, with a very serious disposition. When I was thirteen, in form one, I had to write an essay, "Myself". Bored with giving the stereotypical English textbook essay introduction and after giving much thought about how to portray a real picture of myself, I cheekily started my essay with this line: "I was an ugly duckling that grew up into … an ugly duck." I guess that goes a long way to reveal my sentiments about marriage at that time.

I was always a serious person, focused on study and success. My primary days were in an all-girls school, where I stood out as the head prefect of the school—which said something about the authoritative side of my nature. With close friends, I was friendly, even mischievous at times. But with others, I was reserved and, perhaps, even to some, quite intimidating.

It's not that I didn't know how to smile but that I was blessed with very straight lips. No matter how I smile, they can only curve upwards so much. It was always either people would see me with a serious face, or I would be laughing my head off. Laughing was only between close friends, so that did not leave me with much other choice unfortunately.

My entire young life was always driven by a need to succeed, and I worked hard to get whatever I wanted. Naturally, I still had many things to reach out for in my young life then. Marriage did not quite fit into my agenda in life at that time.

I wonder today if my serious disposition was what triggered the ESRD—because I did not know there were other important things in life.

Was that why I had kidney failure? This was a sudden unexpected experience—the only setback to all my dreams and ambition at that time.

And then there was the strange fever I had.

I had it twice, what I called the 'black urine' fever—once when I was fifteen, whilst in boarding school, and the other time when I was in my final year of study in Salford. Both times, the symptoms were the same—a short bout of very high fever and a general feeling of malaise, leaving me feeling lethargic. And I would pass out black cloudy urine. Even from back then I had always suspected that my urine was stained with stale blood, thus the black, cloudy appearance. However, both times I kept the incident to myself. Truth be told, I think I was afraid I would get admitted if I went to the hospital. At fifteen, I did not want to trouble my parents with trips to clinic and medication bills to fork out. Still, I sensed even then, that the symptom was a tell-tale sign of a significant illness (although I did not in the least suspect it would involve my kidneys).

Maybe I just did not want to find out the truth because I was bent on pursuing my ambition and did not want anything to stand in my way. Maybe I was merely praying and hoping whatever it was that was afflicting me would eventually go away. When I was fifteen, my father did take me to a clinic to treat the high fever and earned me a week's leave at home. When I was in my final year of university, I just let the fever run its course and for my body to cure itself. I guess my previous experience with the fever had desensitised my anxiety and worries.

Yes, the fever did go away each time—unchecked and silently.

So, I wonder if this strange fever that made me pass out blackish urine was what brought about my ESRD.

Was this why I had renal failure?

I was always a thin child, and later I grew up as a slim teenager. Swift on my feet, I was always happy to play sports, especially the track and field events. I was even once nicknamed "the Scrambler" by some boys in school. Physical education was my favourite subject—anything for a jump and run about outdoors. History followed next. And in my senior years, it was biology. Yet, despite my energetic activities, I was often down with colds and running nose. On certain days during my early teens, I would be sneezing almost every morning for no apparent reason.

With regards to food, my picky attitude was not only confined to my choice of fruits, but I was fussy over other foods too. I did not like spicy food, and when I was a child, bread was all I could tolerate for breakfast. Every evening, I would wait for the "roti man" (bread man) to buy my supply of homemade bread. I was his faithful customer. Thinking back, I recall he was an Indian Muslim probably in his mid-thirties. One day, as usual, he was cutting the bread into slices when he started making small talk.

"You like bread very much, don't you?" he asked me, to which I gave a definite nod.

"So why don't you follow me back to my country and you can have all the bread you want all your life?"

I was only nine! He must have been joking, I am sure. But to a mere child at that time, that was enough to scare the life out of me.

Things changed when I got into boarding school. Every time we were served vermicelli for breakfast, I would find myself struggling to finish it. Back then I believe I would only eat vegetables if my life were threatened at knifepoint. Bland dishes like soup and rice porridge did not meet up to my palate either. I have always found them too watery. I was, and still am, more of a gravy person. Sadly, most of the food at the boarding school at that time leaned more towards the bland side.

Above all, the worst part of my eating habits must be this—I totally disliked drinking plain water. My drinks had to be sweet all the time, hot or cold. Besides that, coffee was (and still is) an absolute *no* for me. Drinking coffee would bring about an almost immediate reaction—runny nose, purging and vomiting, and tearing of the eyes—all simultaneously. Unfortunately for me, in the boarding school, coffee was served at almost every breakfast and teatime. I can confess now that, since I don't drink coffee and I did not like plain water, I usually ended up not drinking anything at all.

So, I wonder if my finicky eating habits were what brought about my ESRD.

Was this why I had renal failure?

I will never know.

It was the end of the year. Christmas was fast approaching. Everyone was in a merry holiday mood. The Arndale Centre in Manchester was usually packed with Christmas shoppers around this time of year. The weather was getting cold; it had to snow soon. And so, with the joyful "ho-ho-ho" spirit, one could feel the cheerful ambience all around. Perhaps it was because of this too that my supposed date of admission into the Salford Royal Hospital for a renal biopsy was postponed to the following year, 1984.

Christmas was a quiet event for me. And that made it a good time to reflect.

I remember a verse in the Holy Quran, when Maryam, or Mary, the mother of Jesus (peace be on him) cried desperately to God as her moment of childbirth drew nigh:

> And the pains of childbirth drove her to the trunk of a date-palm. She said: "Would that I had died before this and had been forgotten and out of sight." (Mary [Maryam] 19:23)

With my impending renal failure at that time, I felt I could well understand what Maryam went through. What trials and tribulations the mother of Isa (Jesus) had to go through—to suffer the ultimate pain of labour alone at so young an age. But she had endured, and God had rewarded her most generously with eternal paradise.

I looked into myself. What were my hardships compared to that suffered by Maryam, mother of Isa? I only had to contend with my physical problems; but the blessed mother of Isa had to face abuse of her dignity, her chastity, and the upcoming birth of a most blessed son at such a young age.

Who was I then to complain? Her patience and perseverance inspired me. I was determined to pull through this. My body may have been afflicted with an illness, but as long as I believed that God was only testing me, my spirit would hold on.

Still, debilitating thoughts crossed my mind. I was worried I would be weakened by my illness and that I would become dependent on others. I was and still am, I believe, quite fiercely independent, and I do not fancy the thought of having to depend on others for my existence.

Even worse, I never wanted to become a burden to anyone else.

A lifelong invalid.

A liability.

From an early age, I had told myself that having a good education was my ticket to being independent—study hard, get a good job, earn a good living, and be master of my own self. I had strived for that, spending the most part of my life in pursuit of a good education and scoring good grades. I was just a few months away from graduating and fulfilling my dream in life. I had not counted on falling seriously sick. It was just not in my scheme of things. I began to worry about imposing on other people's lives if they had to take care of me because of my illness.

How was I to deal with that?

Strangely enough, it was at this time that my good friend Siti confided in me. "Fizah, there is this brother who is looking for a wife before he goes home to Malaysia—final year student … like you. He has seen your picture and is interested to pursue. Would you be interested enough in him to consider marriage?"

Oh God! As if I had not enough headaches of my own already!

CHAPTER

3

Honour the Name

*Sometimes when things are falling apart,
they may actually be falling into place.*

Spring was in the air; I was engaged.

It was just a simple understanding between my then suitor (later husband) and me. I am ashamed to admit today that, when I first came to England, I was just a young woman with the Muslim tag to my name. By this, I mean that I bore a Muslim name, observed the five daily prayers, and fasted in the month of Ramadan, but that was about it. I was not in touch with Islam; I had no personal attachment to the Islamic way of life. I had always honoured my religion of course, but I'd never really looked inside me to understand what it meant to be a Muslim—at least not until I came to England, ironically enough. I can safely say that I was enlightened about my faith in Islam when I was in England, a country where Islam is the minority.

Seeing the Western way of life made me question mine—especially when I started questioning how I, as a Muslim, was any different from the non-Muslims.

Especially in how I dressed. At that time, I would normally just dress in blouses and pullovers and sweaters or cardigans over a blouse or shirt and jeans. I would wear a snow cap, and that would be my crude way of covering my hair. How would that indicate I was a Muslim? Adult Muslim females are supposed to wear a head-dress and cover most parts of their bodies, except the face and palms. With my dark skin tone, and the way I dressed (very unlike a Muslim woman), anyone could easily have mistaken me for a non-Muslim Jamaican.

In Islam, standards of modesty call for a woman to cover her body, particularly her chest. The Quran calls for the women to "draw their head coverings over their chests" (Light [An Nur] 24:30–31).

Prophet Muhammad (peace be upon him) instructed believing women to cover their bodies except for the face and the palms. The clothing must meet the criteria of being loose enough so as not to outline the shape of the body and thick enough so as not to be seen through.

The overall appearance should be dignified and modest. In other words, Muslims should look like Muslims.

I realised I had some soul-searching to do. The first of which was, I began to dress as a true Muslim would, headdress and all.

In the United Kingdom, I witnessed the free mixing of males and females. The young people around me were more prone to show their affections in public—holding hands and hugging and kissing, sometimes amorously so, as I once witnessed while having an early morning stroll in a park in Grantham.

Being in the United Kingdom among a totally different culture than the one I came from made me think of my presence here on earth as a Muslim and the responsibilities incumbent upon me as a Muslim. I knew from the holy Quran that there was no compulsion in Islam:

> Let there be no compulsion in religion: Truth stands out clear from error. (The Cow [Al Baqarah] 2:256)

However, once a Muslim, the responsibilities and obligations need to be obeyed in totality. After all, that is the meaning of Islam itself—to surrender oneself to the will of God:

> O ye who believe! Enter into Islam wholeheartedly; and follow not the footsteps of the Evil One; for he is to you an avowed enemy. (The Cow [Al Baqarah] 2:208)

So, when the way I dressed before, the way I behaved, did not in any way indicate that I was a Muslim, how then was I any different from the non-Muslims?

Was my verbal proclamation that I was a Muslim enough, without any responsibilities and obligations?

It was these thoughts that challenged my intellect. Penitence followed, and I started studying my religion with more purpose and diligence and slowly began to adhere as best as I could the tenets of Islamic fundamental principles.

I learnt that one of the Islamic codes of life is that of segregation between the sexes. Islam does not condone free mixing of the sexes. When a woman comes of age, it is preferred in Islam that a marriage is arranged for her with her safety being the main interest and also to protect her chastity. However, it should be noted that there is no compulsion upon the Muslim woman—the woman is free to accept or reject any suitor who anyone might arrange for her. She is free to choose for herself.

And so, in the United Kingdom then, it was common practice among us Malaysian Muslim students to be matched with each other by close friends who were already married—an arranged marriage for the sake of God and to protect one's faith for whosoever wished to do so.

Turning fully into Islam changed my perception of marriage. I accepted it as a sacred pact in seeking God's favour. I was still hesitant about being married before I finished my studies, but I knew once I got back to Malaysia, I would probably not meet anyone who shared my aspirations in Islam. That would be a big problem for me.

My husband and I had met at a common friend's house, who had proposed the arranged meeting.

The meeting was set for us on 26 March 1984. Siti had arranged a meeting between my future husband and I at her house in Cheetham Hill, where she lived with her late husband, Muha (may he rest in peace; he passed away a few years back due to kidney complications). They would be our chaperone throughout the meeting.

The twenty-minute bus ride to her house gave me a lot of time to think—particularly, about my father's strange letter which arrived just a few days prior. It was strange because, for the first time ever, the mention of marriage had cropped up:

> I met a long-lost relative recently and we got talking. He expressed his wish to bring the family closer. He has a son and was wondering if I had any daughters eligible for marriage.

I thought of you. Are you okay to consider marriage? I would very much like you to think about this. You will be graduating soon and coming home anyway. For your information, his son is also a graduate and is now working as a health inspector. He is several years older than you.

For the love of God. What timing!

I remember sitting at my desk for a long while staring at the writing pad, contemplating how to reply to my father's letter. His question had taken me by surprise. I felt awkward discussing marriage with him. I must thank God that He had laid down the principles of marriage in me, and I told myself that I would stand by those principles.

Dear Abah (Father),

With regards to your proposal of marriage on behalf of a long-lost relative, I have given it much thought, and for the moment, this is what I can say.

Over the years I have been in England, I have become somewhat closer to my religion and hoping to live my life seeking the pleasures of Allah. And I realise that, to do so, the man who is to be my husband must share my aspirations as well. I do not know this nephew of yours at all; I have never met him to know his views of religion and the Muslim family.

So, since you have met him, suffice it for now for me to ask you if he prays the five daily prayers

and if he fasts in the month of Ramadhan. And
one other important thing for me to know is,
does he smoke?

This matter of marriage proposal never had the chance to
see daylight again.

At Siti's house, my husband-to-be and I sat facing each
other a distance away, where we made the *taaruf* (introducing
oneself to the other) with Siti and her husband as chaperones. It
was just a simple introductory meeting with the intent of getting
to know each other and asking questions about each other, even
some personal ones. It was truly the strangest meeting of my
life.

"How many siblings do you have?"

"What do your parents do?"

"What does Islam mean to you?"

"What are you looking for in your spouse?"

"What are your hopes for your children?"

Those were the "his" questions.

"Do you mind a working wife?"

"What are your aspirations for Islam?"

"Do you have any inherited illness or genetic defects that I
need to know about?"

These were the "hers" questions.

There was no need on my part to ask about prayers or if he
smoked. I trusted Siti enough to find me someone who had no
problems with obeying the five tenets of Islam. She knew too
that I never quite favoured anyone who smoked.

"It would be difficult to convince my children the dangers
of smoking if their father smoked," I'd once argued.

Both my husband and I were in our final year of study, and
neither of us was keen to be married in Malaysia at that time,
where tradition commanded that there should be the *bersanding*.
This basically meant that we would be put on display for all to

come and watch, sitting demurely on the altar—a non-Islamic practice. My husband had never seen me except for a candid shot that had been shown to him. I, on the other hand, had never seen him at all. The taaruf was a way of finding out if we were compatible in any way. Love could come later from mutual respect for each other. We both believed this, as God has promised this in the Holy Quran:

> And of His signs is this: He created for you
> helpmates from yourselves that ye might find
> rest in them, and He ordained between you love
> and mercy. Lo! Therein indeed are Signs for folk
> who reflect. (The Byzantines [ArRum] 30:21)

For both of us, we found out from the meeting that we shared the same common views about marriage, and more importantly, we had the same aspirations for Islam. I guess that was the factor that sealed our decision to be married to each other.

During the taaruf, I made it a point to make him truly understand my health condition. I explained to him my imminent renal disease and the dire consequences I might be facing. He seemed to be able to accept it at that time.

(Later I found out that he had no idea what I was talking about, but as long as it was not inherited, he did not mind anyway.)

When the taaruf was over, and after both of us had had enough time to contemplate being married to each other, I performed the *Istikharah* prayers repeatedly to seek guidance from God and to help me make my decision. It turned out that he too made his prayers before we finally decided to accept God's will to tie the knot. To this day, I do not understand what he saw in me. The son of a retailer, he is tall, fair, and good-looking if I may say so. He was a student in Sheffield University, studying engineering. During the meeting, he appeared large. But I found out later that it was the parka he was wearing that made him look huge.

Actually, for me, the Istikharah prayers were performed even before I met him—when I was considering the idea of meeting up with him. The Istikharah prayer is a short prayer, which is performed to seek God's guidance in making the right decision in any matter—in this case, my marriage decision. Since it can be repeated as many times as one thinks necessary, that was exactly what I did, praying hard that the decision I made would bring blessings in the end. Although it is permissible and encouraged in Islam to meet up and have a good chaperoned talk with a possible candidate for marriage, I never really fancied the idea of meeting up with any guy to discuss personal aspects of my life. It took me several prayers before I finally decided to meet him.

The last prayer was performed one night before I went to bed. Still in ablution after the prayer, I was pulling the covers over me in bed when, for no apparent reason, I suddenly sat up and uttered the word "Fikri" and the state "Terengganu". Mystified, I ignored my strange outburst and went to sleep.

I had a dream that night—of a very fair man wearing glasses and smiling at me.

The first thing he said when we first met was, "My name is Zulbahri" (which seemed to rhyme with Fikri) "and I am from Terengganu.".

Even though he was not wearing glasses at our meeting, I found out later, and much to my delight, that he was short-sighted and actually wore glasses. I have always admired men who wear glasses. The glasses give them a look of serious intellect.

A few days after the meeting, Siti came over to inform me that "Brother Zul" had proposed. With the continued Istikharah prayers I had been performing, I felt strongly in my heart and mind that I had no reason to reject his marriage proposal. Still, the moment I said yes, I felt a sudden heaviness in my heart—perhaps due to the realisation that my carefree days as a single individual were numbered.

I never met up with him after that until our actual wedding day, a month later. That about summed up my romance story with him.

Once the decision was made, Zul, as my husband is called, then went on to make a phone call to my father back home in Malaysia to ask the latter's permission to marry me.

"You have my permission to marry my daughter in England, but I have this one condition. Please do not stop my daughter from completing her studies," Abah had said.

My father knew only too well that, once we were married, my husband would have the ultimate say over me. His request that I finish my studies moved me. It reminded me of the high hopes and the faith he had in me. I can only thank God that, despite my illness, I have not failed him and his wish for my success in my studies. To me, my personal wishes will always come second to my parents' dreams and hopes for me. I can never repay what they have done for me—ever. I know my success in studies was mainly because of their prayers for me. No requests from them were too much for me.

A bit about Abah, my father.

He was a schoolmaster; strict but open-minded, he was a temperamental but passionate individual. It was easy for him to lose his temper, but he could cry just as easily too, especially where it concerned family matters—us, his children. Once when he visited my oldest sister who was admitted into hospital for an appendicitis surgery, Abah cried to see her in the green hospital gown. Apparently, it pained him to see his children in such condition.

I never really knew what made my father give his consent through the phone, even before checking my husband out first. I would like to think that it was my father's trust in my judgement. Or perhaps it had something to do with the call I had made earlier.

For more than three months, I had kept my medical condition secret from my family back home. However, when my husband proposed and we agreed to be married in England, I knew I could not hide my illness from my parents any longer. They had to know that one of the reasons I wanted to be married in England was so that I would have someone to care for me in the condition I was in at that time. Sadly, until today, I question the wisdom of my decision to inform my father of my illness.

When I broke the news of my renal condition to Abah, I was surprised that he sounded cool and composed over the long-distance phone call. He told me to take care and not to worry about things too much.

That went well, I thought.

Alas! What I did not know then was that perhaps the shock of hearing about my poor health, and with me being so far away from home, was too much for him to bear. Not long after, my father's legs buckled under him, and he suddenly could not walk again without crutches; later he was in a wheelchair, which lasted until the day he passed away in 1991.

And that was why, regardless of my illness or my upcoming marriage, I had to pass my finals and return with a degree scroll. My father's words of advice when I first went to boarding school stuck in my mind never to be forgotten.

He had said, "I don't have any riches to pass down to you. The only wealth I have that I pass to you now is my name. Be proud of it and make it your personal responsibility to honour the name you carry."

I never forgot those words all those years when I was in school and then at the university. It was a driving force in me, to

excel in my studies. That was all I could do to show how much
I appreciated my parents' sacrifices for me. And I was not going
to let my illness stop me from getting my university degree and
making my parents proud of me.

By the end of March 1984, it was study leave for us final
year students. I was engaged by then, after having agreed
upon a spring wedding in late April, just before the finals
and just before the fasting month of Ramadhan commenced.
Meanwhile, my kidneys continued to deteriorate. I was still
heavy on the painkillers.

Wednesday, 4 April 1984, I checked into the Salford
Royal Hospital, scheduled for a renal biopsy—my first ever
hospital admission. Friends accompanied me to the hospital.
Once I'd been warded, the doctor in charge had to run
extensive tests on me. I was an Asian, so, just as in my first
appointment at the outpatient's clinic, the doctor wanted to
know as much as possible about my background—even my
geographical background. To me at that time, I thought it
felt quite condescending initially. He asked me if I lived in a
house with electricity, if I had tap water supply in the house,
if I lived in an attap house or in a building with good sewage
system. I found it strange and insulting. Of course, I did! I'd
always had electricity and tap water in my house for as long as
I could remember.

It was much later that I finally understood the logic and
even necessity behind those questions. It was during the time
when I went back to my husband's hometown in Terengganu
upon our return to Malaysia. When I visited his relatives in
the more rural area, I needed some time to adjust to the very
unfamiliar dialect they used. Then, almost in a sense of déjà
vu, one of the aunts started asking me about my parents' home

in Klang, Selangor, which was about an eight-hour drive from Terengganu at that time.

"Do you have electricity where you live?"

"Do you get tap water supply in your home, or do you still fetch water from the well?"

"Do you have an indoor toilet, or do you use the latrines outside the house?"

I was speechless for a moment, and then realisation hit me.

Those aunts had asked me all those questions for another reason. Back then they had only just gotten electricity supply into their homes. Even then, not all homes enjoyed that privilege. Many still had to use water from the well for drinking and bathing. I must admit, in the beginning, I had some challenging and frustrating moments attempting to adjust to the compromised condition. The toilets were outside the house, and that proved among the biggest challenges for me; I was self-conscious all the time taking my bath. And God forbid I should get a stomach ache in the middle of the night!

I realised then that, having lived in a town all my life, what I had taken for granted was a luxury only some could afford at that time in other places. I finally understood why the doctors in Salford Royal Hospital needed to question me that extensively. They probably wanted to exclude meagre living conditions as a probable cause for my deteriorating renal condition.

Back in the Salford Royal Hospital, it felt strange to be in a ward where all around me were English people—foreigners. Or was I the foreigner? It was uncanny that, my first time ever that being admitted into a hospital ward had to be in a foreign hospital, surrounded by foreign people. At that time, I was sure most of the patients in the ward (mostly elderly ladies) had never seen a Muslim woman up close. I was sure I looked strange enough wearing my headdress all the time. We Muslims pray five times a day. One good thing about my faith is that I do not require any special place to offer my prayers to God. What is important is that the place is clean and that I face the direction of the Holy Kaaba in Makkah when I offered the prayer. That was easy enough to determine using a compass.

And so, when it came to prayer time, I could feel all eyes on me. I am inclined to believe none of them had seen a real live Muslim praying in full attire before. I can only say I was glad that it was the twentieth century (and long before the 9/11 tragedy), and people were generally courteous enough to respect my rights, even though at that time none of them talked to me at all. My guess is that they probably could not figure out if I could understand them at all.

Later in the day, a young female doctor came up to check up on me in preparation for my renal biopsy the following day. I knew she had asked more questions than necessary, presumably to satisfy her curiosity about myself as an Asian. She was slightly shocked that I was 22 years of age.

"Goodness! I thought you were 18," she exclaimed.

She was even more shocked to learn that I was still a virgin when she asked my permission to do a vaginal examination on me.

"Owh, okay. I promise I shall be very careful," she said gently, trying to appease my worries.

I must say I was glad she respected my status and took extra precaution as she proceeded to examine me.

"Hmm, very convincing," she remarked when she was done.

To this day, I would like to believe I was a learning experience for that pretty young medical officer.

The next day I was taken to the surgical room for my renal biopsy procedure. Even though I had fasted from 12 a.m. the night before as instructed by the night nurse, food was furthest from my mind at that point in time. Once again, I am thankful to the doctor for taking time to explain the procedure in a way I could understand. Only then was I made to lie down on my front, preparing to have a tiny piece of my kidney drawn out to find out what was wrong with it.

The room was warm enough, but I remember shivering—certainly more in fear than the cold. Even though I understood mostly everything the doctor had told me, to imagine the needle piercing my back and right into my kidney was not something easy for me to appreciate.

All bashfulness disappeared and self-consciousness evaporated when I felt the doctor give a shot of the anaesthesia into my back. It hurt, needless to say—and then there was a numb sensation. The numbness took away some of the anxiety. But still, how I wished at that time there was someone to hold my hand and comfort me. Then the doctor told me to breathe in deeply and then hold my breath; and suddenly I heard and felt a slight thud on my back. I guess that was the needle piercing my back into my abdomen and slowly sliding right through my left kidney.

At first, I could not feel anything much, but after three or four tries, I could sense a blunt aching on my back, and it was getting more and more difficult to hold my breath for any length of time.

There was only the doctor and me in the surgical room; if there were others, I cannot remember. At that moment in time, I have never felt more alone, all by myself in a foreign land, so far away from my parents and totally under the mercy of an English doctor. It was a humbling moment of truth for me. I remember the silent tears that managed to escape my eyes, not so much from the pain but more from the feeling of sheer helplessness, totally under the mercy of a stranger.

Procedure completed, I was sent back to my bed, the furthest in the ward.

"You need to lie down on your front for the next several hours okay, dear," one of the nurses told me kindly. "Try not to move much."

It was really uncomfortable to be pinned down in that manner with no movement allowed.

Ignorantly, I prided myself that, whenever it became inconvenient to use the toilet, I would not feel like going to the toilet. As it turned out, I did not realise I was actually connected to a catheter and that I was filling up the bag with urine and some blood because of the procedure.

Unfortunately, as the anaesthesia wore off, the back pain became quite unbearable. It felt heavy, like someone was sitting on my back, so much so I had to request a painkiller. It took the greatest effort to stop myself from crying again in front of the other patients in the ward. But what was even more frustrating was that I could not even perform my prayers the proper way. Still, the beauty of my faith is that, when conditions are less favourable, we can offer prayers to God in whatever way is available to us. Thus, in the situation I was, prayer was offered by just mere thoughts (*niat*) and lying down, with no ablution, as I could not move. But I respected the prayer times and devoted that time to the remembrance of God. I would do the proper prayer once I on my feet again.

I was reminded of the saying (Hadith) of the Holy Prophet Muhammad (peace upon him) as narrated by Imran bin Husain who had said, "I was suffering from haemorrhoids [piles] so I asked the Messenger of Allah, peace be upon him, and he said, 'Pray standing; if you are not able, then sitting down; if you are not able to do so, then pray lying down'" (on the authority of Bukhari, Abu Dawood, and Ahmad).

After twenty-four hours of lying on my front, a nurse helped me turn on my back. I was thankful to God to find myself comfortably mobile without too much pain. The bleeding in my urine had stopped too. That evening, I decided to stretch my limbs and walked over to the common lounge to watch some TV programme. I remember feeling rather hesitant and smiling nervously as I joined the other patients already seated around the coffee table. Clearly, I was the youngest in the lot, as I took my seat at the furthest end and listened to the elderly ladies as they made small talk. I was pleasantly surprised as one of the ladies offered some cookies.

"Here, love, would you like some cookies?"

As I mouthed my thanks, one of the other ladies started asking me questions.

"Where are you from, dear?"

"Are you a student at the university?"

One even complimented me on my use of English. "You speak very good English. That's very encouraging."

"Are you a Muslim?"

It is sadly ironic that, at that time, in the early '80s, many people had no idea where Malaysia is, but when I pointed out that it was sandwiched between Thailand and Singapore, the *oohs* and *aahs* immediately followed. I guess people were more familiar with Thailand and Singapore from way back then.

One lady expressed her surprise that I was actually 22 years old then. She thought I was 'not a day over 17'. How about that as a compliment to boost one's ego and morale? I simply had to smile at that. They seemed impressed. It was a comforting feeling to know that they accepted me and that they all had kind and encouraging words for me upon learning about my renal condition. I was grateful for their friendliness. I guess illness brings people together, regardless of age, race, or colour.

And once again I am reminded of the words of God in the Holy Quran:

> And among His Signs is the creation of the heavens and the earth. And the difference of your languages and colours. Verily, in that are

indeed signs for men of sound knowledge. (The
Byzantines [Ar Rum] 30:22)

After three days in the Salford Royal Hospital, I was
discharged. I had gone through the whole procedure—the
endless blood tests, the urine tests, and the renal biopsy to find
out what was actually wrong with my kidneys. Most of the tests
were inconclusive, but one thing was for sure—both my kidneys
were diseased, and the basic cells, the nephrons, were damaged.
I was told that I had glomerulonephritis. The prognosis was
not good.

CHAPTER

4

"Say Yes, Please"

The best things in life ... are not things.

The finals were drawing near. And so was my wedding day. The one-time meeting with my husband-to-be followed by several nights of the Istikharah Prayers had helped me a lot in accepting my husband's proposal of marriage. Together we had decided on a spring wedding, 21st April, a month away from the upcoming fasting month of Ramadhan and from our finals.

I had just been discharged from hospital, and I was back to the same condition before hospitalisation; the headaches still attacked me frequently. But I must say that I managed to run my life fairly steadily and kept myself busy. Apart from my routine hours of studying, it was time to make arrangements for my wedding; I wanted it to be a simple but meaningful event. That had always been how I imagined my wedding to be. It was decided that the wedding would be held at the Cheetham Hill mosque in Manchester, and my husband would come over from Sheffield. I can only guess that my husband, through his friends in Manchester, had handled the arrangement and booking for the use of the mosque and of the Imam who would conduct the *nikah* (exchange of marital vows) as well. Everything seemed to be going smoothly and how I envisaged my wedding should be, except for one small flaw—none of my family members would be attending my wedding. Neither would his.

Personally, at that time, I was at a loss as to what to prepare for the eventful day. My mind was still solely focused on the condition of my health. God be praised, my housemates and close friends at the university soon took over the wedding preparation, despite their busy schedule for the upcoming examination. One friend, Sheila, was kind enough to make me a pink baju kurung to match the maroon *songket* (traditional cloth woven from gold thread) my parents had given me previously. Others had offered to prepare dishes and desserts for the *walimah* (small ceremony following the exchange of wedding vows where guests are served food and drinks to announce to the community that one is married). Meanwhile, I was busy buying bed linen and some stuff to decorate my room and make it look more homely. It was something that helped take my mind off from my worries about my health momentarily.

On the eve of my wedding day, my friends gathered around in my room and prepared me for my big day. My new pink dress hung prettily in my cupboard, the room was made up with flowers, and cards posted by my family were put up on the wall.

Later my friends applied henna on all my fingernails, as was customary for Malay brides. I watched as they dyed my fingernails with the lovely orange brown colour of henna.

I remember not getting much sleep that night. Habibah or someone asked me how I felt.

"I don't know. It's strange. I feel calm actually," was my honest answer.

Perhaps the impact of the event had not really sunk in, I guess.

There was not much excitement, just a certain quiet calmness.

Maybe it was because I was alone, with none of my family members with me. Earlier in the morning I had received a few mails from home—my siblings and nieces and nephews had written to wish me happiness on my wedding day.

Inevitably, though, little things that happened amid the hustle and bustle kept reminding me that my health was slowly deteriorating.

It happened one night while I was watching Sheila as she prepared my dress. She was a skilful self-taught tailor, although at the university she was training to be an engineer. She had bought herself an electric sewing machine, presumably as an investment to help her make some money when friends came to ask her to sew their dresses. The sewing machine had a foot pedal that we only needed to press down to get it going. While Sheila was cutting out pieces of cloth, I offered to help her sew a few parts of my dress that she had previously cut out and pinned together. More than really wanting to help, I was actually curious to try the machine myself.

I don't know what really happened, but I guess it was all the vibrating that went through my back as I pressed on the foot pedal and the machine started to stitch the cloth pieces together. At first, I simply ignored the discomfort I felt in my back as I pressed on, but after a few moments, it just got too uncomfortable and nauseating.

"Are you all right, Fizah? You look pale," I recall Sheila asking.

I could not catch any more of what she said. What I do remember was rushing out of her room and making it just in time to the toilet bowl before I began to throw up furiously. When my friends learnt about it, they were adamant not to let me lend a helping hand with almost anything else after that. That ended all my attempts to help around.

The wedding at the Cheetham Hill mosque was a simple yet merry one. Friends from around Manchester and Sheffield came as guests. The mosque, at that time, was modestly built—the upper floor, which housed the main praying hall, was where the male guests were placed. The female guests were on the lower floor.

During the nikah, the imam, a Pakistani, came down to ask me if I agreed to the marriage.

"Sister, Brother Zulbahri has asked for your hand in marriage with a dowry of a gold ring worth seventy pounds. Do you accept his hand in marriage?" he asked.

This was the defining moment of my life. I was about to change from a spinster to a married woman.

I was petrified.

I could not utter a single word.

Now, it is told in one Hadith of the prophet (peace be upon him) that a woman's silence when asked that very question could be accepted as her consent (on the authority of Bukhari and Muslim). I was praying that the imam would understand that was exactly what my silence meant and spare me further ordeal. It was at this point that the imam did something that totally took me by surprise.

He came up close to my ears and whispered, "Say yes, please."

Taken by surprise, I could not help the smile that escaped my lips.

But what came out from my lips was the most timid, dry whisper of "yes"—just enough for the imam to hear.

And when he asked me to put down my signature on the marriage certificate, it came out as the tiniest scribble I could have ever made—a testimony to the extent of my nervousness at that moment. To this very day, it has become the object of jest for my husband. He would never let me forget what a "ridiculously tiny signature" I penned down on our marriage certificate.

I am grateful to God that, even though my family was not around and even though it was just a modest occasion, I felt blissfully happy and blessed. The ceremony went well and just as I had always hoped my wedding to be—without pretences and vanity. I could feel God's blessings in the simplicity of the event. I could not have asked for anything more.

With the nikah completed, the guests were served a light meal of fried vermicelli and some cakes and puddings. It was at that time when one of my seniors came up and touched me lightly on the shoulder. I was with my friends, watching them eat. I was just too worked up to get anything into my stomach.

"Fizah, your husband is waiting for you outside. He is ready to get back to Sheffield," she said smilingly.

Husband! The word sounded so foreign to me at that time. I nodded, got up, and got into my coat before I went out through the back door.

Nervously, as I stepped out of the mosque, I was overwhelmed to see a group of Malay men, all bearded and in their thick jackets, standing on the walkway. To my shocked horror, I immediately realised that I could not recognise my husband amid the crowd of men. After all, I had met him only once before. A moment's panic seized me before I managed to calm myself down enough to think rationally. Any of those men who would remove himself from the crowd to come and get me must be my husband.

True enough, after what seemed to be like the longest embarrassing moment of my life, standing alone and feeling silly, my husband, Zul, walked up to me, gave me the salaam, and asked if I was ready to leave. He was dressed simply in white

Malay *baju melayu* with grey slacks—so simple that of course I could not single him out as the bridegroom.

The drive from Manchester to Sheffield seemed to last forever. One of his seniors volunteered to drive us from Sheffield with his wife and child in the car. At one point, I started to panic, wondering what I had gotten myself into. Heck! I didn't even know the people in the car. I got so worked up that I even contemplated asking the senior to stop the car and running back to my safe haven in Salford. That was how terrified I had become.

But it turned out I was not alone in this. Later my husband would tell me, "Glad it's over. I was really anxious during the nikah."

When we were finally alone in his home, he gave me a large computer printout of my first name, "Nor".

"I could not sleep last night. Nervous maybe. I was thinking of you the whole night and what I was to embark on." He laughed nervously. "So, to distract my mind, I ended up with this printout with your name on it. Here, take it," he said, smiling at me.

And from that day on, I was no longer alone—I was one of two. Although he was only a weekend husband during the remaining days of our stay in the United Kingdom, we used the time to get to know each other better and to learn to live with each other.

It was awkward in the beginning. One early morning walk at the Weston Park in Sheffield finally broke the ice. We were at that time staying in the house with another married couple. And when we returned from the walk, we realised he had forgotten to bring his key. We were both reluctant to wake anyone from the house so early in the morning to let us in. It would be too embarrassing. So, we stood looking at each other and started laughing at the desperate situation we were in. As my husband's body shook with laughter, he knocked into the door, and all praise be to God, the door was suddenly pushed open. It turned out that the door was not even locked. Both of us praised God profusely as we quietly crept back into the house.

On another occasion just a few days after we were married, we were waiting for a bus when my husband spoke out. "Can you look at the number on the bus for me? I forgot to bring my glasses."

I had never seen him in glasses. I was not even aware he was short-sighted. It may sound strange, but to learn this of him pleased me so much. The vision I'd had after my Istikharah Prayer—that of a bespectacled man smiling at me was true after all.

In no time, we got to be very close, and it hurt every time he had to return to Sheffield after visiting me in Salford for the weekend. I had forgotten how it was to be on my own before and not to have him around.

There is something beautiful and sacred in falling in love after marriage. We were free to explore each other's mind and body without restrictions and guilt. In Islam, sexual intercourse for the sake of God between husband and wife becomes an act of worship. There were always new things to discover about each other. In the back of our minds, we never forgot that our marriage was for the sake of God. Whatever imperfections we saw in each of us, God would suffice.

As for me, God's words cannot be denied. We got married for His sake. The love did indeed come into our hearts just as He promises in the Holy Quran:

> And of His signs is this: He created for you
> helpmates from yourselves that you might find
> rest in them, and He ordained between you love
> and mercy. Lo! Therein indeed are Signs for folk
> who reflect. (The Byzantines [Ar Rum] 30:21)

CHAPTER

5

Of Big Lizards and Bad Dreams

Life goes on.
Probably not the way you wanted it to be,
but always the way it's supposed to be

November 1984

I was already back in Malaysia for over four months—a biology graduate and a wife to my husband. All praise to God who had helped me all the way in my effort to obtain a degree scroll in honour of my parents.

What was unfortunate was that, whilst I was home for good, having completed my studies, my husband had another year to complete his studies and had flown off back to Sheffield in October. It was hard to be separated after being together for the last three months. Still, there was a sweet moment to it when, later, my husband told me about it.

"I was just feeling so sad at leaving you behind that I spent the first part of the flight just closing my eyes and trying not to cry," he confessed later.

Meanwhile, I did nothing about my renal condition whilst I was living with my parents. Being among my parents and siblings helped me cope with my husband's absence and eating mom's home-cooked food made me forget my illness. My twenty-third birthday, the first after marriage, was spent without my husband beside me. There was no special celebration, just a fun one made by Liza, one of my nieces who my parents had taken care of from birth.

"Look what I baked you," she proclaimed proudly. She was only nine at the time, and as she approached me, I realised she had "baked" me a cake made of mud and leaves. Not to dampen her excitement, we finally had a mock birthday party—another touching memory.

And so, after a four-month break of just living the easy quiet life at my parents' home, I finally received a letter to proceed with my postgraduate teaching course—a one-year course in Maktab Perguruan Temenggong Ibrahim, a teaching college in Johor.

So, my bags packed, I was off once again with my faithful companion Habibah, boarding the train to Johor Bahru in pursuit of our career. The course we were about to attend for one year was the first of its kind run for overseas graduate students who were on the Ministry of Education scholarship. Sadly, the syllabus seemed as if they were prepared on the spur of the moment; they seemed haphazardly arranged with no clear-cut objectives. At one point, we were even made to attend cooking lessons.

Rationale?

So that we might survive wherever we were to be posted to later on.

Ironic actually—given that we were all away overseas living on our own for the past five years at least, fending for ourselves. If only they had given a thought as to who did our cooking for us all those years we were away from home.

Initially, time seemed to move rather slowly at the college. It felt strange to be living with friends again. Habibah, along with another friend of ours, Normah, and I managed to rent two rooms in a house near the college. We were graduate students and not eligible to stay on campus. In between classes and assignments, I missed my husband a lot. To take my mind off things, I would get the first bus home every Thursday after class—a six-hour journey at that time—and reach my hometown by 9 p.m. Abah would be waiting for me at the bus terminal, accompanied by my big brother Aral. I would spend the weekend in the comforts of my parents' home before returning to Johor Bahru on Saturday morning. Class started on Sunday in Johor at that time.

The slow rambling life continued for nearly one semester until somewhere in mid-July when my husband joined me in Johor. He had completed his studies. And whilst he was waiting for his posting as an engineer, we decided he would stay with me. By then, I was doing a six-week teaching practicum stint in Benut, Pontian, one of the provinces in Johor.

For the teaching practicum stint, eight of us had been sent to different schools in the area, and I was assigned to a school in Benut, the place farthest from the town of Pontian, together with two other friends who were going to teach chemistry and mathematics. Initially we had planned to stay somewhere near the school in Benut. None of us had any form of personal transport and staying far from the school might pose a problem.

We forgot one thing. In a small town such as Benut, at that time, there were not many houses up for rent. The day we registered we spent the night in the home of a lady who was teaching at the primary school. She saw us wandering around dragging our luggage behind us and took pity on the three of us, offering her home, which she rented with another friend. Just like that, an unspoken bonded feeling developed between teachers. God bless her soul!

The headmaster of the school told us of two houses he knew of that were empty at the time. One was exactly beside the school.

What sheer good luck, I thought.

Alas, my relief was short-lived.

"I would not recommend that large house to you young ladies. The house is haunted, and I am not making it up. Many have seen and heard strange things going on over there. I don't think you ladies will last long in that house," the headmaster explained.

The three of us looked at each other. It was a unanimous decision that we were not going to take any chances.

"There is this other house," the headmaster continued. "It's a small *kampong* house, with one room. If you ladies would like to see it, I can contact the owner to take you to view the house."

That sounded promising. So that evening, the owner came after school hours and showed us the house. Earlier we had decided not to impose on the Good Samaritan teacher longer than was necessary. Her room was hardly large enough for her, let alone to have the three of us cramping up her space. So, we graciously said our thank you and goodbyes and took ourselves out of the modest house.

To our shocked dismay, the house for rent turned out to be more like a lone hut in the middle of a field of tall weeds.

I was speechless. The house was decent enough I suppose, but it was in the middle of nowhere. And it looked as if it had not been lived in for quite some time. Unfortunately, it was already too far into the evening to back out. We would not have anywhere else to stay for the night if we did not move in. Rohana and I knew we had no choice.

But not Lina, our chemistry teacher friend. She had decided to return to Johor Bahru and to come back the next morning. There was no way she was going to spend even one night in the hut. Yes... to be honest, a hut describes it perfectly.

That was it. To return to Johor Bahru was not solving any problems. It was only delaying things momentarily. Rohana and I really had no choice actually. We decided to rent the place. After all, the landlord had waived off the deposit, and the rent was actually quite a bargain.

Before he left, the landlord handed us the keys. "By the way, there is something you should know. There will be no electricity for tonight. There is a small concert tonight, artists coming, singing, you know. They usually use up all the electricity," he said as he turned to leave.

Great. In the middle of nowhere and no electricity. Could things get any worse?

They could... and they did.

The house was small; the lower portion housed the kitchen and was made of cement. Small crudely built stairs led to the upper lounge made of planks with one tiny room at the corner. The toilet was just outside the house but connected to the kitchen. Still, one had to get out through the back door to get to the toilet.

"Right, then, we had better settle in quickly before it gets dark. Good thing you brought candles with you, Rohana. What made you bring those candles?" I asked, curious.

"Intuition I suppose," she replied. God bless her for her intuition.

We agreed to sleep in the hall together and stored our luggage in the small room. When night came, we lit four candles and placed them in the four corners we had cleared and placed our pillows and spread the bed sheets. The landlord was right; there was no electricity that night.

I remember both of us sitting on the plank floor hugging our knees and making small talk whilst waiting for the Isha prayer—the last prayer for the day. In the distance, we could softly hear a band playing, someone singing and claps and cheers when she finished.

"You know what, Rohana, we don't know how long this house has been empty. Why don't we recite some Qur'anic verses just for protection?" I suggested. And so, after prayer, we sat down together reciting the Holy Quran.

We had made our toiletries earlier on; none of us was too keen to have to go outside in the middle of the night. We even had a very early dinner and drank very little to avoid such possible toilet emergencies in the middle of the night.

It had been a very exhausting day, so thankfully both of us fell asleep while the night was still young. It had started to drizzle when I dozed off, and it was a cool breeze that blew through the house that night.

Somehow, I was awoken from my slumber in the middle of the night when the candle at the top of my head burnt itself out. I woke Rohana up to ask for another candle, which she had set aside on her side of the pillow. After lighting it, I went back to bed.

I was once again awoken later in the night. This time it was a deep ferocious growl that woke me up. As I sat up to listen better, I realised that the hall was dark; two of the candles had died out. It was pitch-black and eerily quiet.

The growl frightened me. I still remember it made the hairs on my arms stand. It sounded so close—and so menacing. Immediately, I lit up two more candles and set it near our feet. The growl immediately stopped. I turned to look at Rohana. She was awake too.

"Did you hear that, Fizah? What is it?" I could hear the fear in her whisper.

"It's stopped now, Rohana. I think whatever it is, it's been scared away by the light from the candles. Don't worry, we just have to make sure the candles continue to burn." I know I was comforting myself actually.

I remember very clearly the fear that gripped me. Lying down again, I can still recall the thoughts that ran through my mind.

What was that thing? It sounded so close. Is it a demon? A robber? Or worse still, a wild animal?

Will the local people hear us if we are attacked?

Just as precaution, if it were a demon, I started reciting verses from the Quran that I remembered by heart. I firmly believe now, as I did then, that the verses would drive away any demon that might want to disturb us. Still, the raised hair on my arm would not come down.

Then another thought passed through my mind that made my heart stop and gripped me with fear. If it were the demon, verses from the Quran would chase it away. If it was a human with evil intentions, there was still hope that Rohana and I might overpower him or at least plead with him not to harm us.

But what if it was a wild beast? A large lizard perhaps? No amount of pleading would stop it from attacking us. The thought got me worried. I was even more determined to stay awake and remain alert. Rohana was keeping very still and quiet, but I was sure she was thinking the same things too and too scared to even make the slightest sound.

Somehow, the thoughts and the recitation must have lulled me back to sleep. When another growl woke me up, I saw that the hall was pitch-black, and the growl sounded so near, almost at my feet. I jumped up and rushed to light up two more candles. Just like before, the growl stopped immediately, and there was no trace of any animal around. I have never been more scared in my life. There was no more sleeping again after that.

When the call for the morning prayer reverberated from a mosque somewhere, I knew the worst was over. I turned to Rohana, and she looked worse than she had before we'd gone to bed last night. The way she looked at me told me I looked equally bad.

As I stepped down the stairs to the kitchen below, I was puzzled to see that the floor was wet. I simply could not figure out where the water might have come from but dismissed it anyway. I had other important things to think about—like trying to find a new house. There was no way I was spending another night in this house after last night. I can only thank God today that, as it turned out, Rohana felt the same way too.

"How did you find the house?" The headmaster greeted us when we reached school that morning.

Tired as I was, and forgetting myself for a moment, I relayed everything that had happened to him—even providing the sound effects.

"It was probably a large lizard or an alligator. On occasion, the water level in the swamp does rise, especially if it has been raining, and the animal might have swum into your kitchen," the headmaster said, offering his explanation for the mysterious growl.

Both Rohana and I were dumbfounded.

Now he tells us, I mused.

I just could not imagine what I would have done if I had been confronted by a large lizard. Or worse, I thought of having my limbs lost to one of those beasts. And then I realised, that would have explained the wet kitchen floor.

Until today, I would like to believe that the headmaster might be right—that it was probably a large lizard that had wandered into our hut and not anything paranormal. I can never know for sure. We never went back to that hut again.

Lina came back with good news that our friends (Habibah included) in Pontian town were living in a spacious semi-detached bungalow with four bedrooms and three bathrooms. There was enough space for the three of us. Benut was a thirty-minute drive from Pontian town, but the good thing was there was hardly any traffic in the early hours of the morning. So, the driver who we had made a contract with earlier could make it from Pontian to Benut in fifteen minutes. There would no problem of being late to school at all.

All praise be to God! Our house hunting ended quite well finally.

Since my husband would visit from time to time, my friends were kind enough to let me have one room to myself, whilst my other friends occupied the remaining three rooms. I just had to pay extra rent. And so, my husband would come to visit and stay for some days whenever he could. However, not long after, my husband got his job posting, and it no longer became possible for him to visit me that frequently.

On one of the last visits, he followed me once to the school on a Saturday and waited for me there whilst I attended a school function. During tea break, I went up to him to share some food with him before I went back in again.

Now at that time, I was slowly losing weight and was more on the thin side. At the end of the programme, one of the administrators called me up to have a private word with me. I was shocked when, without even thinking to ask me, he accused me about conduct unbecoming. I was stunned.

"What do you mean?" I was bewildered by his accusation.

"It is not 'proper' that you should bring your boyfriend to school. You should be more discreet and show some respect to the teachers here. This is not the big city," he explained. I thought he looked smug saying those words.

I was taken aback. I suppose I shouldn't really be so surprised as, prior to that day, the particular administrator had not even taken the trouble to get to know us trainee teachers. But to blatantly accuse me like that was definitely uncalled for. (There are always those "I-am-holier-than-thou" characters in our lives, aren't there?) I wanted so much at that time to act out the defiant teacher, just to spite him further. But my rational mind reminded me that I could not let my family name be marred by such outrageous accusation. So, although feeling a bit peeved at his holier-than-thou attitude, I patiently and politely explained to him that the "boyfriend" was actually my legally wedded spouse, and I had my wedding certificate to prove it.

I guess he felt embarrassed after the initial shock and quickly went on to explain his actions—citing that he thought I looked so small that it did not cross his mind that I could be a married woman. I was not convinced by his excuse though. I thought he was just being prejudiced and judgemental.

Still perhaps there was some truth in his words. I was slowly losing weight and not feeling quite myself. In a way, I could feel myself shrinking. I started to wonder if the weight loss had anything to do with my feeling tired and generally unwell lately.

It was at this time, between teaching practicum, attending classes, and going back to Klang over the weekends, that I fully noticed how unwell I felt. I became fussier over my food, and I was feeling sleepy most of the time. This worried me because I prided myself as being a very focused person whenever I attended classes. In fact, Habibah had been worried lately that my kidney condition could be getting worse, and she fussed over me. Yet, somehow deep inside me, I knew it had nothing to do with my illness. Call it motherly instinct, but even before the clinical test confirmed it, I knew that I was pregnant.

It was a tough first trimester for me. For most of the time, I was alone, as my husband was based in Kuala Lumpur and was staying with my parents. Although I felt a very strong motherly feeling permeate me as soon as my pregnancy was confirmed, I was too emaciated to rejoice over my pregnancy. Just to get any food inside me was a torturous ordeal. I simply could not bring myself to hold down more than a few morsels of rice. All I could tolerate was plain cream crackers dipped in plain hot tea.

Still, the sympathy must go to my husband, I must say. Even before my morning sickness started, he was having recurring purging and vomiting for reasons we both could not explain. His suffering lasted for about a fortnight and ceased as soon as mine started.

Then there was one night when my husband came to visit and had woken me up from a dream.

"You are having a nightmare. Why are you crying in your sleep?" he asked. I could sense the worry in his voice.

"I was having a bad dream; someone or something had come to take our son away."

Somehow, I had always felt the baby growing inside me would be a boy. The dream was enough to put the gripping fear in my heart. There was a real reason behind my worry.

Once long ago, my father had told us of a dream he'd had. In his dream, an old lady had approached him and offered him riches if he would give up any one of his eleven children to her.

"There was no way I was going to give up any of my children. I can live without the wealth," he confessed passionately.

I was young and ill—and pregnant too. I was eager and looking forward to having this baby. It is what all married couples dream of. But my failing kidney condition was a constant nagging at the back of my mind. It occupied every minute of my mind. Soon enough, my worry escalated to such a point that even a dream was enough to trigger a panic attack in me.

I believed I had very good reasons to be troubled by my nightmare.

From then on, my condition progressively worsened. By the time I finished my tour of duty in Benut and was back in college, eating became virtually impossible, as everything I ate would be vomited out. I began to worry about my baby inside me and asked my husband to send me to the hospital. Personally, if it were just myself I had to consider, I would not have surrendered myself to the hospital, as I did not fancy the idea of staying in a hospital ward. But at that point in time, I learnt for the very first time in my life that a mother would do anything for her child.

And just in time! I was immediately admitted for risk of ketonuria. I was just not eating enough, almost to the point of starvation (since everything I ate got vomited out) and not getting enough nutrients to sustain the both of us. A little later and my body would have had no choice but to convert wherever there was fat on my body as energy source. I was told that this was considered a medical emergency, and immediately upon admission, glucose was administered into my system via intravenous injection. Once infused with glucose, I literally felt like a flower in bud slowly opening as raindrops hit its parched petals.

And so, by a turn of fate, I was back in touch with hospital life again—this time in the Sultanah Aminah Hospital in Johor Bahru, the capital of Johor. Only this time, I had another life growing inside of me to consider and think of.

During the course of my stay in the hospital ward, I had informed the doctors of my renal problems as diagnosed in England. I was in hospital for a week. When I was finally discharged, I felt almost my old self again. And upon discharge, an appointment was made for me to see a specialist at the hospital.

On the day of the appointment, I had gone on my own again, reminding me of my days in Salford. My husband had just started work in Kuala Lumpur and could not, as yet, take leave to accompany me. It was a long dragging wait for the doctor (Thank God it is faster to see a doctor/specialist today). The long wait left me some time to contemplate the situation I was in and to envision what the future held for me. As a science-based individual, I am trained to look at things objectively and to make calculated and logical predictions most of the time. Thoughts did cross my mind that my progressing pregnancy might somehow aggravate my renal condition. I was in my very early stage of pregnancy. In all probability, the embryo growing inside me had only just become a foetus. In Islam, it is said that the *ruh*, or soul, will be breathed into the foetus after 120 days—four months. I thought long and hard. I knew deep in my heart the dire consequences a pregnancy could cause to my already weak kidneys. I let my rational scientific mind take over.

There is every chance that I might not be strong enough to carry the pregnancy to full term without having adverse consequence to my health. I gave in to my thoughts objectively. *You better brace yourself for any consequences. Be open-minded to any options.*

I had not realised that I had dozed off amid my cogitations until, very faintly and slowly getting clearer, the voice of a nurse calling out my name came into my consciousness. I can recall quite clearly feeling momentarily confused as to my whereabouts. The kind, understanding smile from the nurse was reassuring to say the least. Sadly, my feeling of comfort was only short-lived.

Meeting up with the specialist turned out to be an absolute and downright disappointing experience. I was about eight weeks pregnant, and I was eager to discuss options with the specialist. My mind was set on being objective in all this.

Instead, to my utmost vexation, all the questions the specialist asked me had nothing whatsoever to do with my condition. Instead, when he found out I was attending the postgraduate teaching course at the college, the perhaps forty-something specialist started peppering me with questions about a colleague of mine in the same course I was attending—a young single lady from Sabah or Sarawak; I am not so sure now.

"Is she friendly?"

"Would you say she was soft-spoken?"

"Do you know if she has a boyfriend already?"

For the love of God! What has my colleague in college got to do with my appointment today? Please don't tell me I waited for so long earlier only to be asked these absolutely irrelevant and ridiculous questions. It was simply the most infuriating experience for me and certainly self-degrading for the specialist, in my opinion.

Finally, I got the break I needed and started needling him with questions of my own. I asked him directly the questions that had been uppermost in my mind ever since I'd been warded earlier.

"Is it clinically okay for me to keep this pregnancy?"

"What possible complications may happen to my pregnancy in my present state of health?"

"What do I need to do to maintain maximum function of my kidneys during my pregnancy?"

I was prepared to discuss any possible options if I had to.

His answer?

"You have nothing to worry about. To maintain your kidney functions, I suggest you eat 'one damn egg' every day."

I swear in the name of God Almighty those were his very words.

The paradox of his statement, which kept reeling in my mind was that I had learnt in my final year of study that, when the kidneys are diseased or impaired, protein was the first thing that should be cut down. Yet here was a specialist who was telling me to take "one damn egg" every single day. I was baffled and confused. All I could do to pacify my doubting mind was to tell myself that the man was a specialist in his field; he must surely know what he was talking about. I was just, at that time, a first-time mother-to-be in her mid-twenties.

What did I know?

So, with the health of my baby uppermost in my mind, I did exactly what the doctor ordered. I ate one damn egg every single day.

I should have trusted my motherly instincts.

By the time November 1985 came, I had finished my one-year course in Johor and was back in Klang with my husband. Due to my health, I continued to stay with my parents whilst I waited for my first teaching posting. I was still having my morning sickness, but the pregnancy seemed to be progressing well without much fuss. I was eager to continue with my follow-up to chart my progress. My cravings had started too. Once my brother had taken me for breakfast at a *roti canai* stall (roti canai is a kind of thin Indian prata bread) with butter for added flavour, and that soon became my constant craving. My husband at that time had not gotten his driving licence yet, so I would get up very early in the morning and follow my brother when he sent my sister-in-law to the school where she worked as a teacher. The stall was located close to the school. Bless my brother. His wife was pregnant too at that time, just a few months ahead of mine. My big brother was literally looking after two pregnant women at that time.

I am not one who believes in mere coincidences. In my opinion, everything happens for a purpose—at either the right time or the right place. I am grateful to God; in my case, it was both. It just so happened that, at that particular time when my kidneys were deteriorating, an uncle of mine, who I'd never known previously, by the name of Dr Prohoeman from Indonesia and a renowned specialist in nephrology, was on a tour of duty at Kuala Lumpur General Hospital, the GHKL. With this information in mind, my father thought it would be a good idea for me to meet my uncle and seek out his advice. I am forever indebted to my uncle for using his influence to make arrangements for me to receive treatment at the hospital. After all, the nephrology department at GHKL was fast becoming one of the most advanced departments in the Asian region at that time. (My uncle passed away a few years ago, may God bless his soul and give him the best rewards. I am thankful to God that I managed to visit him in Bukittinggi, Sumatra, to introduce my children to him and let him know I was doing fine post-transplant before his demise.)

It was through my uncle that I got to meet the top nephrologist, Dr Abu Bakar (now Tan Sri Dr Abu Bakar). I handed him all the documents and test results from the Salford Royal Hospital. I never really knew why, but from henceforth, he would refer to me always as "the Salford Girl". However, as soon as I told him I was in my fifth month of pregnancy, he seemed uneasy with the information. Firmly but gently, he told me that my pregnancy could not be continued.

"The pregnancy will aggravate your kidney problem. You cannot carry on with the pregnancy."

What? Terminate my pregnancy?

When I can already feel him growing inside me?

And what of the specialist in Johor Bahru who told me I could keep my pregnancy?

"The specialist I saw in Johor Bahru told me that my kidneys would not be affected by my pregnancy, and he said to eat one damn egg every day," I argued with Dr Abu Bakar.

He just shook his head but did not say anything.

This was absurd. The hell I was going to give up on my baby now. I had prepped myself to be open-minded; in fact, I was open to suggestion when my baby was still early in his foetal stage. But not now! I was dead set on keeping my baby.

I was adamant this time and simply refused to listen to what Dr Abu Bakar had said. God bless that wonderful man. He was the epitome of the word "patience" itself. Far from admonishing me for my outright obduracy, he admitted that perhaps I would like to speak to his colleague first. So, immediately I was referred to Dr Zaki in room 2.

Dr Zaki was as soft-spoken as Dr Abu Bakar. Yet somehow, it was the way he presented the case—putting the words in a plain and matter-of-fact manner, no beating about the bush. He even said that my practice of taking a lot of proteins had probably aggravated the kidneys. I grimaced angrily, thinking of that specialist in Johor Bahru. However, Dr Zaki's honest and down-to-earth explanation seemed to make sense to me. Or at least it made me agree to think and reconsider what he was suggesting.

"Terminate this pregnancy or risk endangering your life. Those are your two options," he had said pointedly. His words jolted me to the harsh reality of my condition.

Or perhaps it was simply that the reality of my condition was slowly sinking into me.

More level-headed then, I said, "I am not the sole decision maker in this whole matter. I need to consult and discuss with my husband."

To me personally, my husband, Zul, would be the ultimate decision maker in all this sorry state of affairs.

"I understand. Talk it over with your husband first. If need be, ask him to come here so I can talk to him and explain your present renal condition." I nodded, and immediately Dr Zaki hastened to add, "I hope the two of you will make your decision as soon as possible. Let's meet again in a month's time."

Returning home, I struggled with the task of delivering the bad news to my husband. How should I tell him that we might possibly have to terminate this pregnancy—that there would probably be no baby after all?

Before we returned to Malaysia after our studies, on a whimsical mood, my husband and I had gone shopping for some baby stuff—clothing, shoes, blankets, a baby carrier, and even baby feeding bottles. When we found out I was pregnant, we had excitedly opened the box where we kept those things safely and started unpacking them. And now I had to tell him this!

I thought long and hard, amid the tears that simply would not seem to stop. I was desperate for an idea of how to convey this sad news to him gently. My mind was numb. I could not imagine his reaction. Even though we had gotten married at an early age—he was only six months older than me—both of us had always shared the same dream of starting a family as soon as possible. My husband was not much of a talker then, just as he is now, and he was always a bit slow to grasp any matters that concerned my health whenever I told him about them. I needed someone to consult, someone who would understand my dilemma. This was something too heavy for me to bear on my own. I knew my husband would be devastated. I had to break it to him as gently as possible.

I sought my big brother Zafik. We were kindred spirits, the both of us having lived away from home once when we were in school, and I knew I could talk to him about the quandary I was in. When I told him of my plight, he was speechless for a moment. He was not married yet at that time, but we all came from a family who loved children.

What I clearly remember from our heart-to-heart talk was his confidence that my husband would understand.

"Your health must come first, sis. Zul will understand," he had said honestly.

Comforted and reassured by my brother's words, and with what little strength left in me, that very evening I sat down and wrote a letter to my husband. I knew I would not be able to tell him verbally. I would surely break down. I told him, as simply and as clearly as I could, what the doctors had told me. I reminded him that, whatever that we thought was ours was not final and that everything came from God and would ultimately return to Him.

"I love this child that is growing in me so much; he is very much a part of me now. I am ready to accept any possibilities— any decision that you make. If you choose that I should carry on with this pregnancy, I will. I mean it. God will give me strength."

That was how I ended the letter. Somehow, deep in my heart I know now that I was hoping he would make the decision to keep our baby and ignore the doctors' advice.

Later that night, when he had read the letter, he seemed calm enough as we talked.

"We'll consult what Islam says in this matter first before we make our decision alright?" he said matter-of-factly. The one admirable quality about my husband is that, while he can get irritated very easily when his egg is not perfectly half boiled, (which can lead to spoons hurled halfway across the kitchen), he can be very patient in times of adversity. For that, he has earned my respect many times over. And again, when faced with this heartbreaking dilemma, his opinion was that whatever Islam decreed in this matter, we should stand by that, whether we liked it or not. And God willing, He would help us. I agreed, feeling a sense of deep comfort and peacefulness knowing God would know best.

Before the scheduled appointment with the doctors, my husband decided to meet up with one renowned and respected Muslim scholar and health practitioner, the late Prof Harun

Din (may God bless his soul and place him among the pious), to ask his expert opinion on what Islam had to say for a case such as ours. I felt a sense of relief that my husband was taking charge of our plight.

Meanwhile, my baby was fast growing inside me.

CHAPTER

6

Abdullah

You have to do what is right for you.
Nobody else is walking in your shoes.

I was well into my twentieth week of pregnancy. After completion of our teaching course, some of my friends had gotten themselves temporary employment whilst waiting for posting. My parents had suggested I just stay home with them considering my state of health. My husband agreed with them.

It was one lazy afternoon when I felt a strange and distinct pulling and tugging inside me. Worried and wondering if my state of health was affecting my baby, I voiced my concern to my late grandaunt (may God bless her soul and place among the righteous) who frequently came to stay with us.

She looked at me knowingly and then replied casually, "There is absolutely nothing wrong with your child. The baby is kicking you from inside."

Oh my God! Her answer stunned me and brought mixed feelings. It was such an awesome sensation. Suddenly, I felt this renewed surge of love for my baby—the feeling so overwhelming that my heart felt like bursting, and my body felt warm all over. I cradled my tummy and imagined myself cradling him in the crook of my arms. I knew my baby was a boy. During the last visit to the maternity clinic, the obstetrician had run an ultrasound scan and determined his sex. I smiled to myself. This was one spunky baby I had inside me, kicking away from inside his mother's womb.

And just as suddenly, too, I sobered up as I remembered the outcome of my husband's meeting with the professor. He had informed us that, in the Islamic faith, in situations such as was in my case, when there are two lives to consider, one alive and one whose life is as yet uncertain (as was my unborn child), it becomes imperative to save the life of the living.

How can I?

How can I possibly give up on my baby now?

True, his kicks were only just feeble twitches. But to me, I felt he was as much alive in me as I was. I was his mother—no mother would give up on her child. At that point I would rather give up my life if there were any chance at all that my son would live. My heart was being ripped apart. The professor had told that, if God so willed, there would be other children once I was treated and cured. However, if we insisted on my carrying the baby, and should I die because of it, then that would be a life lost and the end of my generation; and that would be, in itself, an injustice. My husband was satisfied with the professor's explanation. He decided that we would adopt the principles of the second Caliph of Islam, Umar Al Khattab (Allah be pleased with him)—which was that we were actually just moving from one fate designed by God to another one of His will.

Yet when I felt my baby move, I knew nobody would understand the overwhelming feeling of love that only a pregnant woman can feel. Even if I lived through all this, and if I had other children after this, each one would never be the same as my firstborn. I knew I was willing to die for my son. I was his mother; born or unborn, he was my son; and all the love there was in my heart was for him. No sacrifice was too great for my firstborn. How could I give up on him? How could I?

22 January 1986

My husband and I were now living in Petaling Jaya. I was a newly appointed teacher teaching at Bukit Bintang Boys' Secondary School. I was twenty-four weeks pregnant.

On that date, my husband and I finally made our way to the Nephrology Department at GHKL for our long overdue appointment with Dr Zaki, to discuss our decision regarding my pregnancy. We had delayed our decision long enough. As soon as I registered my name at the counter, the staff nurse told us not to go anywhere. Perhaps she had been informed earlier about my case, and she did not want me to be in the waiting room long enough to change my mind; I can only hazard a guess. True enough, in no time at all, my name was called out, and I was summoned to room 2.

As if understanding my troubled state of mind, Dr Zaki turned to my husband and addressed him first. I was relieved that he had decided to mediate the meeting.

Dr Zaki was quick to cut to the chase. He started off by asking us if we had come to a decision.

Unsure how to begin, my husband paused and stammered a bit before asking.

"I would like to know first if there is any other way to treat my wife without having to give up on her pregnancy?"

Dr Zaki stared at me with a questioning look. I stared blankly back at him. Somehow, I would like to think he understood.

He turned to my husband and patiently began to explain. "I am sure your wife has explained why I wanted to meet both of you today. Your wife is suffering from end-stage renal disease, which is, right now, aggravated by her pregnancy. I don't think, in her condition, she can carry the pregnancy through to full term with all the toxin that is building up in her. Continuing the pregnancy will surely only endanger her life. But I am sure you already know this."

There was a momentary silence as both of us contemplated Dr Zaki's words. What I can remember was that my mind was blank—a numbness taking over my soul and mind. It felt as if it was not me Dr Zaki was talking about.

I watched as my husband nodded his head slowly before he finally spoke. "We have decided to save my wife. We will do as you advised. We will stop this pregnancy."

I cannot imagine how difficult it must have been for my husband to say those words. But both of us had prayed long and hard for God to help us decide. We had done our Istikharah prayer many, many times. And we believed this was what God had ordained for us. We both have faith that there was always a blessing behind anything that befell us. We remained forever thankful, no matter what.

I recall clearly my siblings' reactions when we spoke of our decision. My parents, especially my father, fully supported our decision. It was understandable; I was his child. Some of my sisters thought that I was not showing full trust in God (*tawakal*), taking the future into our own hands.

"How do you know that the doctors are right? Why don't you put your trust in God and just continue with your pregnancy? Let God decide. What you are doing now is taking things into your own hands," one of my sisters had reproached me.

No, we were not sure. Neither my husband nor I knew what the future held. But what we did know is that we were putting our full faith in God no matter what the future held by what we decided on that day. We had done our prayers for guidance, and we had full faith that whatever was in store for us would be the best for us at that time. God may not give what we want, but He would surely give what we need.

Prior to this, my grandaunt and my oldest brother had suggested traditional options. Rest assured, we had exhausted all options and resources. Sadly, things just did not turn any better. The renal profile continued to show that my condition was inexorably worsening. We simply had no choice.

I never minded what my siblings had to say. They did not understand. It was enough that I knew it was way out of my hands. It was enough that my husband and I knew we were doing it in God's name, and He knew what was in our hearts. I knew I loved my unborn son (and still do and will always until the day I die, when I hope to meet him again, God willing). I knew my husband felt the same too. He had always wanted a son who would uphold the cause of our faith; yet now he was giving up on one. We both knew the agonising pain of making that decision; and we were leaving our fate and our future purely in the hands of God. The one comfort we held onto at that moment were the words of Sayidina Umar (God's pleasure be upon him) on matters concerning fate — "that we were moving from one fate of God to another fate of God".

"We have delayed this long enough; the foetus is entering its twenty-fourth week. From now on, its growth will surely affect your wife's health. I will refer you to the O&G department for an immediate TOP" (termination of pregnancy).

Dr Zaki's voice sounded distant. This was all like a dream to me—a long bad dream that I could not seem to wake up from.

(One friend told me recently that he's addicted to his children. Anyone who holds this same point of view will surely know that, when any one of our children precedes us to meet his or her Creator, a part of us dies too. The void will never to be replaced—no matter how many children we may have after that. And for this reason, this memory stands out so clearly in my mind.)

My appointment for termination of pregnancy with the O&G was made for the very next day—straight for admission. There was no more delaying. In retrospect, maybe that rush was a blessing in disguise too. The rush left me no time to think and feel the pain that gripped my heart.

By eight in the morning of 23 January 1986, I was back at the hospital and was seen by the specialist—a mild elderly Indian gentleman.

"We will give you something that will cause your uterus to contract and expel the baby," he explained gently.

I remember asking him anxiously, "If the baby comes out alive, you will try to save him, won't you, please?"

The doctor had looked at me long and hard. I remember then he let out a slow sigh before he spoke, "Do you know why you are having this procedure done and what the probable outcome is?"

I simply nodded. I just felt that I needed to say it, nonetheless.

He looked at me a moment longer before he spoke again gently to me, "All right, of course. If the baby comes out alive, we will try our best to save him."

That was all I asked for.

I was placed in a two-bedded room, sharing with a young Chinese lady. We made some small talk, but I knew I wasn't much for conversation at that time. As soon as my husband left for work, a nurse came in and administered an injection. I do not know what the content was. But almost immediately, I felt strange inside me, followed by a feeling of intense chill that forced me to lie down and pull up my blanket. Yet I was still shivering. I struggled to call the nurse and asked for an extra blanket. She returned with a few blankets and covered me up, but I was still shivering uncontrollably, so she added another blanket on me and then yet another.

It was at that moment that I felt my baby inside me suddenly turn and toss violently—I can only imagine today that he was writhing in agony—as I felt the wave of contraction in my womb. I pushed away at the blankets to look at my abdomen. It was moving in all directions, which only confirmed that my son was in huge discomfort, perhaps even in great pain. Desperate and desolate tears came rushing down my face, as I placed my hand over my abdomen, as if by gently massaging my tummy, I could comfort my child inside me. There was no stopping the torrent of tears at that point. All I could do was to cradle my tummy and whisper hoarsely, "I am sorry, my baby. I am sorry … so sorry … so sorry."

On that day I finally understood what true sorrow meant and how deeply hurtful sorrow felt.

The contractions lasted for a short while only, but it seemed like a lifetime. I felt it would never end. Eventually it slowed down and stopped, and my baby quietened down. The intense cold I'd felt earlier disappeared, leaving me utterly exhausted.

What went through my mind at that time?

A sense of sheer helplessness.

A sense of absolute loss.

A feeling of being terribly alone.

As I drifted off into an exhausted slumber, I gently stroked my baby from the outside and spoke quietly to him, "If you can fight, baby, then fight to survive, my son. But if it is too difficult, then just let go. I love you so much, and I am terribly sorry for putting you through this, for causing you so much pain. Please forgive me, my son. Please forgive me."

The whole procedure was repeated at around twelve noon, and I had to go through the ordeal all over again. I admit I cried openly and broken-heartedly as I felt my son struggle once again inside me. But somehow, his movements were not as strong as the first time. The following injection was due around six in the evening.

At around five that afternoon, my husband came to visit after his office hours. He sat at the edge of the bed near my feet and listened as I recounted quite incoherently, amid tears, what had happened earlier. As he leaned closer to hear my tired voice, suddenly a gush of water burst from me, splashing onto his shirt. My water bag had burst.

"What is happening? Where is this water coming from?" he cried out.

Panicked, my husband rushed out to alert the nurse. I knew immediately I was about to go into labour. Dr Amir, a young doctor on call, arrived soon after and helped me with the delivery. I was so grateful that he was supportive and comforting, encouraging me gently all the way as I steeled my heart to accept that my pregnancy was coming to an end and as I gradually found myself unable to control the urge to push. My emotions were raw at that moment. The feeling of having your very being wrenched out from you against your will left me in a flood of tears, and I have no recollection at all of the pain of delivery.

When the doctor handed me my stillborn child, I just could not stop the tears. Yet at the same time, I must admit there was a sense of pride and amazement that this little bundle was perfect, and he was beautiful. He was fair skinned and had a birthmark around one of his eyes, just like his father. His tiny and frail little fingers had separated, no longer webbed. He looked peaceful, almost as if he was sleeping. It was a strange feeling—a mixture of sheer helplessness and pride at the same time. It is a complicated thing; it is difficult to have just one emotion at one time.

And so, on Thursday, 23 January 1986, at 6.23 p.m. —in the Muslim calendar, 12 Jamadil Ula 1406—my first child, my first son, who my husband and I named Abdullah bin Zulbahri, meaning "the Servant of God", was born—still and lifeless.

Goodbye, Abdullah, my son. Wait for me in heaven, God willing. To me you are a martyr—for you have given up your life so that I may live. I regret that I have no picture taken of you, but your fair skin, like that of your father's; your long slender fingers; and that birthmark on your eye, exactly like your father's remain permanently etched in my memory. When you were brought back to the house of your *atok* (grandfather) Manaf, it was your uncle Pak Aral and your auntie Mak Mok, my elder brother and sister, who bathed you. You were so small and fragile that they had to place you in a vegetable colander and gently drew water over you. After that, your Atok Manaf insisted we use his *ihram* white cloth as your shroud.

Did you know that the caretaker of the cemetery near our house was kind enough to allot you a tiny space out of sympathy? Everyone loves you, Abdullah, and your uncle and aunt kept saying how much like your father you looked. Your father told me later that, on that night, whilst your Atok Manaf kept vigilant guard over you, he curled up alone on the bed and sobbed his heart out for your loss, hugging his knees to his chest, seeking solace he could not find.

And did you know that, after I was discharged from the hospital, I went to stay at your grandfather's home just to be near you? One day it rained heavily, and I suddenly rushed out of the house and then stopped short when your uncle, Pak Aral, cried out to me asking where I was going. Did you know my reply, son?

"Abdullah, he will get wet." And then I remembered.

Your Pak Aral just stared when I stopped and just stood in the rain for some time before slowly walking back into the house. I don't think anyone will ever know the void I felt within.

I miss you, my son. Never a day passes by that I don't think of you. Every year, I wish you a silent happy birthday on 23 January. But it's all right. I know you are in good hands. I often dreamt of you when you were a baby. There was always a fair lady zealously watching over you whenever I came to visit you in my dream.

Don't worry about us, my son. Your father and I, we both still ache for you, but we will be patient until we meet again one day, God willing. I take comfort from this Hadith of our Holy Prophet Muhammad, may peace be upon him:

> A woman whose three children die will be shielded from the Hell Fire. On that a woman asked, "If only two?" He replied, "Even two [will shield her from Hell Fire]. (on the authority of Bukhari).

I know even with one.

CHAPTER

7

Downhill Trip

*The reason most people give up is because
they tend to look at how far they still have
to go, instead of how far they have come.*

At 24, I was already a mother, but not quite. I was a mother
who had just lost her firstborn.

A day after the termination of my pregnancy, I was sent for
a D and C (dilation and curettage). This is a procedure that's
usually performed following miscarriages that happen after the
first trimester. In this procedure, the cervix is opened or dilated,
and then any contents of the uterus are removed by scraping the
uterine wall with a curette instrument. For this procedure, I had

to take off all jewellery I had on me. I am not one who is keen on jewellery; all I had on me was my wedding band. And since that day I took off my ring, I have never adorned myself with any jewellery at all—no rings, no necklace, no bracelets, and no earrings. I just could not bring myself to wear any, simply because they would remind me of my son Abdullah every time.

It was not until 2002, that I finally wore any jewellery at all—only because it was a gift from Abdullah's brother, who arrived six years later. He was ten at the time and had used up all his savings to buy me a pendant. It was not even my birthday. When I asked him why, my son Ashraf replied, "Just because I love you, Ummi."

Abdullah's sacrifice had not been in vain. And with my pregnancy terminated, life was back to routine for me as we were before; there was no child to fuss over. Both my husband and I were working by then, and we had moved out of my parents' place to somewhere nearer the school where I was teaching in Petaling Jaya. My husband had rented a small unit on the ground floor of an apartment building.

Unfortunately, the surrounding area looked more like a squatter area. I was not used to staying in such living quarters. Yet there was nothing much we could do about it. Both of us had only just started work, and the rent was what we could afford. Plus, it was the nearest to where we worked. My husband had a point with regards to the distance from our workplaces; after all, at that time the only mode of transport we had was an old rickety motorbike. My husband was on his way to buying a car. So in the meantime, "Old Faithful" (the motorbike) would just have to do. I tried my best to ignore the conditions around me.

Most of the time, my husband was the only companion I had. He would come home during his lunch hour to send me to school, as I was teaching in the afternoon session. It was that old motorcycle that saw him to and from his office and took me to school. If it poured, we would both be stranded for hours. If it did not rain that heavily, we would brave the shower so we could be home as early as possible. We did almost everything together. But there was one thing that he could not be a part of—my illness. That was something I had to handle myself. It was a bit difficult for him to understand how alone and lonely I felt having to bear my illness.

Being sick and alone can very well be the worst feelings of all. I could still stomach the poor conditions of my surroundings, but the loneliness was sometimes simply too overwhelming. My husband, being the quiet person he was, and still is, just watched and listened as I rambled on, sharing my lamentations. He has always been religiously inclined and did not care much for entertainment; we did not even have a television set then. The house, most of the time, was pin-drop silent. Whilst I admit that silence can be inspirational, being in the condition I was in, oftentimes, I would find myself sitting on the floor in the middle of the house, staring blankly at the four walls, frustrated by the deafening silence until I would finally burst into desperate tears.

Most of the time, they would be tears of self-pity; sometimes they would be angry tears. I would be talking to myself, asking myself a thousand questions, berating myself for falling sick. I would find myself asking God why He had to make me sick.

"Have I ever been bad God? I pray the five daily prayers just as You tell us to. I don't speak ill of others. I don't backbite. I have been good. I don't drink. I don't mix freely with men. I have never been to any discos or nightclubs. I cover my hair. I do everything You tell me to. So why do You allow all this to happen to me? Why me?"

These questions would run through my mind again and again until I realised there was no answer that could satisfy or comfort me. The only thing left for me was to accept the situation I was in and surrender myself to God. I began to understand one very fundamental thing. He was the Master; I was the slave. He could do as He pleased, and if I realised my position as a slave, I would realise that my job was to obey. Yet, His mastery was filled with countless mercy and grace. I may be sick, but I was still alive and sound of mind. I may have just lost my son, but I had tasted pregnancy when so many other women could only dream of being pregnant. I realised I had a lot to be thankful for. I should not despair, as God has said in the Holy Quran:

> And do not despair of God's Mercy—only disbelievers despair of God's Mercy. (Joseph [Yusuf] 12:87)

Slowly, I started asking the right questions. Instead of crying my woes, I started asking what really it was that God wanted of me in this trying moment, in this situation.

In retrospect, I know now that God made me sick to make me the person I am today. I had to go through what I went through to really get to know and appreciate God's bountiful love. In the Holy Quran we're told:

> Do men imagine that they will be left (at ease) because they say, 'We believe', and will not be tested with affliction?" (The Spider [Al Ankabut] 29:2)

To hit rock bottom and then to realise you have nowhere else to go but up and to feel God's love as you totally and utterly surrender your fate to Him gives you a perspective on what really matters in life.

Trials are a part of life, and God certainly does not test His servants more than they can handle, as explained in the Holy Quran:

> God does not burden any soul with more than it can bear. (The Cow [Al Baqarah] 2:286.)

I began to embrace the verse—that whilst I was being afflicted with ESRD, it was actually a test from God that was within my scope. It was something God knew I could handle. The confidence this realisation gave me was monumental in itself.

I realised too that, for as long as I was being tried, He was watching me, and He was near. I just had to be patient and place my trust in Him. If nothing else, I knew I was being taught a lesson in patience and forbearance:

> Faint not nor grieve, for ye will overcome them
> if ye are (indeed) believers. (the Family of Imran
> [Ali' Imran] 3:139)

I knew then that my faith, my belief in Allah, would see me through this ordeal. I just needed to affirm my belief—to believe more strongly.

And as I grew weaker, I talked even less—no longer having the enthusiasm to strike a conversation. What I really wanted was to hear people talk and have my little nieces and nephews playing by my side. It was as if their cheerfulness, their happy laughter and playfulness, were therapy for me. It was also simply comforting to be near my parents and siblings. Thus, it ended up that every weekend would find me pleading and cajoling my husband to take me home to my parents' house, about a half hour's drive from my house. At that time, when we did not own a car, I would, on my own initiative, arrange with my older sister Kak Mah to hitch a ride whenever she went home to visit my parents over the weekends. Thank God that, as it happened, my sister and her family made it their weekly routine to visit our parents back in Klang.

Until today I will vouch every time that it would do much good for sick or poorly individuals to have people around them from time to time to cheer them up or just to listen to. It comforts the mind, and that, in its own right, is therapeutic. I am lucky and grateful to God that, most of the time, my husband would oblige without much fuss.

Meanwhile I was back for my routine check-ups at the nephrology department of HKL. At every visit, the doctors would run the renal profile test and the urine FEME. The renal profile is a diagnostic test to collect information about kidney functions. The test requires a blood sample for analysis. In a renal profile, levels of creatinine, calcium, sodium, chloride ions and urea, among others, were checked. From then on, the blood creatinine reading would be indicative of kidney functions and the one I was most anxious to find out every time. Ask any kidney failure patient; his or her worst fear would be to have the reading of their blood creatinine rise.

Sadly, that was what happened to me back then. Every time the results came back, the creatinine reading got only worse. It was at this point that a repeat biopsy was ordered, as the last one performed in Salford was inconclusive.

And so began my association with the hospital again, this time in HKL—starting with a renal biopsy. This time, the results were more revealing, and I began to familiarise myself with the term "glomerulonephritis". Glomerulonephritis is a serious illness that can be life-threatening. It is a type of kidney disease in which the kidney is damaged. It can be caused by problems with the body's immune system, but the exact cause is usually unknown. It's often characterised by inflammation of the glomeruli or blood vessels in the kidney, which progressively leads to reduction of urine output.

Dr Zaki explained later that I was facing the inevitable—total renal failure. The one thing that could delay this impending end was to be very stringent with my diet. I was referred to a dietitian.

When my kidneys failed me, what it actually meant was that my kidneys were no longer able to remove the toxic waste resulting from the metabolic reactions that went on in my body—especially the metabolic waste from proteins that would appear in the form of creatinine. Under normal circumstances, the creatinine would be expelled together with the urine. However, when the kidneys are diseased, the toxic wastes cannot be filtered out, and thus they start to accumulate and circulate in the bloodstream. There is no doubt that their presence can wreak havoc in the head. The only way to remove these toxic wastes would be to undergo dialysis.

And this was exactly what Dr Zaki advised me to do.

What? Surrender myself to the hospital again? I had done everything the doctors had told me to do; I had terminated my pregnancy. Surely, I was supposed to be okay again. What more did they want of me? Had the termination of my pregnancy been futile? I was bitterly resentful at the idea of having my body prodded and poked. Deep down in the back of my mind, the truth was I was downright scared. I did not want to stay in the hospital ward. There had to be other options, or so I thought.

It was at this time that one of my husband's acquaintances, a security officer where he worked, suggested traditional medicine to him. There was supposedly this practitioner who was able to treat cancer and had the advantage of X-ray vision and invisible surgery. I was suspicious. Now, I am not against traditional medicine; it has its merits. But X-ray vision? Invisible surgery? They sounded a little too far-fetched for me to digest. It went against my grain to allow myself to succumb to this unorthodox method of treatment. However, what was more important was that I really doubted the authenticity of his method from the Islamic Syariah (Islamic jurisdiction) point of view. Call it gut feeling—I just did not feel too good about this particular practitioner. Basically, I am an open-minded person; I am of the belief that medicine is not only restricted to the modern, chemically based medicine of today. Yet, this particular practitioner raised much doubt in my mind. There was just something about his ways that did not seem quite right to me. But I needed to respect my husband's efforts.

At this point, one would probably wonder about my husband. A man educated in the sciences; surely, he could see my apprehension. One would probably think he must see the sheer ludicrousness of such method of treatment as proposed by this practitioner. But before anything can be said about my husband, one should try to see things from his perspective. At that point in time, he was a young man with a young wife who was possibly dying of renal failure. Every day he would come home to see his wife getting weaker and weaker and to hear the doctors tell him that his wife was suffering from a terminal condition. I believe he simply felt he had to do something and try out every alternative suggested to him—given that his wife was adamant that she didn't want to return to the hospital. He was twenty-five, an engineer, and men at his age would probably still be out gallivanting and flirting around, single and available, and certainly not burdened with the grave responsibility of a terminally sick wife. One needs only to put oneself in his shoes and wonder if he would not have done the same.

So, I obliged; very reluctantly, as my husband could be equally hard-headed as I was. One of us had to yield. One day, after a few visits to the said practitioner, I decided to do some experimentation work myself. At that point in time, as I grew progressively weaker and more anaemic, my monthly menstruation had slowly trickled to a halt. So, on one of my visits to the practitioner, I decided to let him know of this condition of mine and see what he would be able to see with his "X-ray vision".

The practitioner soon worked himself into a trance prior to starting diagnosis and treatment, transforming himself into an old lady—even sounding like one. I was supposed to be mesmerised by his coming into a trance. But unfortunately for the poor man, my curiosity always got the better of me. And believe me, there was always a flaw that I would catch.

In this trance-like state, the practitioner started to respond. "No menstruation for four months? Let me see ... hmm ... perhaps you are pregnant," he said, if I may add, cheekily.

What?

Wasn't he supposed to have X-ray vision? Couldn't he "see" inside me?

In truth, I knew why I had not had my menses for so long. I was too anaemic to get my monthly periods. My simple experiment had shown to me that this claim of X-ray vision was not really working on me. I was really put off by his cheeky sniggers and remarks, to say the least.

Still my husband told me to give him the benefit of the doubt—that perhaps he was only teasing. It was only out of respect for my husband that I refrained from further protests, allowing myself to be subjected to this ridicule.

Then one day the practitioner treated his patients to a small dinner at his home.

My husband and I had come by sheer chance that night; I think it was because I had run out of the medication he had prescribed. However, I would like to think God was helping me out. I was technically a party crasher, to arrive uninvited and without an appointment. I had no intention of staying at all. We just wanted to get our medication and leave. As I passed by one of the smaller rooms, I saw some roast chicken neatly arranged on plates on the floor. Upon asking one of the women who happened to be there, I found out to my horror that, as part of the feast, he had specially prepared the roast chicken, not for his guests but, instead, for his "unseen ancestors" who'd been helping him with his practice.

Oh my God! What unseen ancestors? That was sheer blasphemy to God. To even be in such a place would be jeopardising our faith. That was it! I pulled my husband out of the house immediately and told him that under no circumstances was I ever going back again.

"That man inside practices shirk to God." I pointed to the house. "He makes feasts to appease his 'unseen ancestors'," I cried out to my husband. "I am never going back there again. It's just not worth jeopardising my faith." That seemed to jolt him.

And that was the last time I ever went to see the practitioner or ever heard of him again.

My kidneys continued to deteriorate. There was nothing to be done by this time but to wait until I got to the critical stage. I am only guessing this as, by that time, the number of renal patients was on the rise, and only the critical cases were given immediate priority. My downward spiral towards the end stage was inevitable. I was on a downhill trip with my failing kidneys.

To ease the burden on my failing kidneys, I was sent to the dietician to learn what I could or could not eat. I discovered, much to my dismay, there was not much I could eat. Everything—the onions, the garlic, the ginger, and the vegetables—had to be soaked in water over night to remove as much of the salt as possible so as not to aggravate my kidneys. I was only allowed a matchbox of protein per day. And I could only drink half a glass of water per day.

I might just as well starve myself.

It was here that Abah came to the rescue. Since I could hardly eat any protein—a matchbox full would mean about just three medium-sized prawns for a day—to spare me from eating just rice without any flavour, he suggested I have noodles and use the miniscule amount of protein as flavour. That way, I could have my protein for the whole day, instead of just one main meal. I did not have much appetite anyway then, so the plan worked out well for me.

As for the controlled amount of water intake I was allowed, once again Abah suggested that, perhaps, I could control my water intake by sipping ice cubes. He went on to suggest that, whenever I felt thirsty, I could just rub the ice cubes over my lips; in that way, the thirst would be partially quenched. I tried it. It worked beautifully. And that was how I managed to keep my water intake to half a glass every day.

Apart from seeing the dietician, not much else was being done for me on the part of the hospital either. I was given mainly Alutabs to curb the gastric-like pains I was having. This is how renal problems go unnoticed, as they often resemble gastric pains and are often misdiagnosed as gastritis. It had happened to me when I was home for the summer holidays of 1983 before I learnt of my renal problems. At that time, my sister Kak Mah had been concerned about my persistent abdominal discomfort and had taken me to see a doctor. The doctor had said it was simple gastritis and had sent me home with some gastric medication. It was only later that I'd learnt the discomfort was one of the symptoms of renal problems.

And so, feeling frustrated at the hopelessness of my situation, I tricked myself into believing that, since my pregnancy had been terminated, I was getting better, and the kidneys would gradually be well again. I did this to such an extent that, when the date came for my appointment with the doctor in view of preparing a plan of action I was to proceed with, I decided to play truant and simply ignored it. Without telling a single soul of my appointment date, not even my husband, I tagged along with my brothers and sisters for a trip to Malacca, a two-hour drive from Kuala Lumpur. Nobody realised at that time how poorly my condition was. Being with my family members on a family activity always boosted my happy endorphins. I was cheerful and was basically feeling good all around.

And I continued with my life as if nothing was wrong with me. Every day, I went to work in the afternoon session. After the termination of my pregnancy, the school discovered that I had renal problems. And because they worried that my illness might interfere with my teaching, I was taken off the teaching timetable and only given duties as a relief teacher. That was quite a blow to me, as I enjoyed teaching and being with the students. Being a relief teacher did not give me much of a chance to build a rapport with the students. As that was my first posting, and I was thus new to the school, being just a relief teacher did not give me any chance to prove myself. Those were frustrating times. I felt useless, unwanted, and redundant. Simply put, I felt I was just a burden to the school. Still, I completely understood the reason for the school's action. They had to think of the students first.

Fortunately for me, I was given a seat in the corner of a row of senior teachers in the school staff room. And given that I was one of the youngest teachers, the other teachers soon mothered me when they learnt of my deteriorating state of health. One of them, Mrs Loh, had a son who also suffered another kind of renal problems, or the nephrotic syndrome. She became very protective over me as well. God bless her. She would be very sensitive to any changes in me and would always advise me, particularly on my diet. Then, there was Mrs Nava, who treated me like her daughter and always kept a watchful eye on me. When I was feeling under the weather on occasions, one of them would generously get me a cup of hot milo drink. I felt blessed to have these two lovely ladies constantly watching over me at school. They were such great comfort. Their concern for me, a newbie in the teaching world at that time, has taught me a potent lesson—the smallest act of kindness is worth more than the greatest intention.

Their kindness inspired me. And to this very day, I strive my very best to help out with young teachers whenever I can. This is my way of thanking them.

CHAPTER

8
—

Surrender

People change and things go wrong.
But always remember, life goes on.

It was just around the Chinese New Year of 1987 when what appeared to be a series of unfortunate incidents led me back to the hospital.

The first one was my sudden craving for durian.

The second was the horrifying hallucinations.

Known as the king of fruits among Malaysians, the durian is famously known for its very strong odour. Whilst many may not be able to stand its strong scent (especially westerners), to me personally, the delicious fruit was something to die for. And

I almost did—literally. Unfortunately, durian is an absolute *no* for ESRD patients. High in potassium, it can almost certainly slow down an already enlarged heart due to water retention from kidney malfunction. I knew that for a fact even back then, but I wonder now why I acted so plain foolhardily.

Was I unconsciously trying to end my miseries by throwing all caution to the wind?

Nothing is coincidental in life; everything has a purpose. I wonder now how I managed to sweet talk my husband, who incidentally detests durians, into buying the most delicious-tasting durian for me with its thick sweet succulent flesh. I began to eat with gusto, as if that would be my last meal.

Alas, after just three bites, I started feeling queasy and a little queer. Most noticeably, I began to have trouble breathing—my heart beating progressively slower—almost laboured. Without attracting too much attention from my husband, lest he reprimand me for my stubbornness, I slowly went to lie down after I had cleaned myself with great difficulty and remained as immobile as I could the whole night.

Back then we lived a simple life—just a mattress, no bed. Honest to goodness, as I lay myself down beside my husband that night, it really felt as if my time was up. My heart's beats were getting distinctly slower and weaker; I could hardly feel them. My chest felt tight and heavy. It was as if I was being sucked from the inside into a dark and deep abyss. I felt very cold, unable to move. It was not a sensation that was easy to forget.

Strangely enough, there were no feelings of regret as thoughts of dying crossed my mind. There was no fear either, just a sense of extreme fatigue and melancholy. It felt as if I had walked a very long distance, and all I wanted to do then was take a rest, to surrender to a deep sleep. If my life ended that night, I was just sorry I would not get the chance to say a proper goodbye to my husband, my parents, and my siblings.

Quietly, I crossed my arms over my chest, closed my eyes and quietly mouthed the Kalimah Syahadah—the declaration of the Muslim faith. "I bear witness that there is no god but Allah, and Muhammad is the Messenger of Allah."

If I were to die, let me die in faith to Allah.

I have no recollection of what happened after that.

I know until today my husband never knew that I was preparing myself for death that particular night.

"Wake up ... wake up ... Its Subh prayer time." My husband's voice sounded dim and distant as he shook my body to wake me up.

Was I still alive? I woke up with a gasp, not unlike the desperate gasp for air after being under water until you reach the edge of your limit of being without air.

"Alhamdulillah, all praise be to Allah," I muttered quietly to myself.

God knows how grateful I was that I had survived the night's ordeal. Gingerly I touched my arm; it felt warmer than it had the night before. A pang of self-sympathy rushed through me as I noticed how small the diameter of my wrist had become. I was getting very, very thin, the skin dry and dull. Then I realised that I should be rejoicing the fact that I was still alive after being quite sure I was going to die the night before. I tried to get up, and immediately the room started to spin around me. I was still too weak, but that was quite all right. I was still alive for one more day. I had survived the night, although I doubted I was anywhere near getting better. Getting up and walking ever so slowly like a very old lady, I laboured through the morning Subh prayer.

And then it dawned on me. I finally realised I was at the end of my tether. There I was, weighing only thirty-three kilograms, just a mass of bones covered in dry, listless, and wrinkled dark skin; yet my legs still could not carry me. My heartbeat was terribly slow, simply refusing to beat any faster. The grim truth of my reality was later honed into me when the postman came to deliver the mail at 11 a.m. The simple act of walking to the front gate just a few metres from the front door proved to be the most laborious task I ever had to perform. I was gasping for air with every little step I took. Things were really getting out of control. I knew I was very near the end.

When my husband returned home in the afternoon to check in on me, I voiced out my anxiety, careful not to mention the events that had happened earlier. I did not want to hear myself say it aloud – maybe deep in my heart; I was not really ready to go yet. I begged my husband to send me to Kak Mah's house in Damansara Utama, not too far from my place.

He complied, and that evening, together we rode the Old Faithful to her home. The old motorcycle could only allow us to travel so fast, so as we cruised over to my sister's house that evening, I remember distinctly looking around me. The sun was setting, so it was a nice bright orange in the sky. It was still sunny but no longer hot. Cars and other vehicles were rushing beside our rickety old motorcycle. It was just buzzing with life on the road. The wind blew against my face as I hugged my husband from behind. We did not talk along the way; I was preoccupied looking around me. When we stopped at the traffic lights, I watched as people walked briskly on the sidewalk. There was a restaurant near the traffic lights, and I could see it was bustling with life—people talking with each other, children running and playing. There was just so much life.

Any moment, my life could be taken away from me, given the condition I was in. There was no sadness and no fear; I just looked and wondered if I would still be around tomorrow, next week, or the next month. I just watched everything pass by me as we rode off to my sister's house.

As it turned out, my husband decided to stay the night at my sister's house before leaving directly for work the next morning. I did not realise he had packed his clothes earlier.

My decision to spend the night at my sister's house must have been God inspired. I believe it was the most correct decision I have ever made—for two reasons.

The first was the call from my husband the following evening. He was calling from our home.

"O my God … our house … we have been robbed! The house is in chaos," he shouted almost incoherently across the phone.

My heart stopped. Cold fear gripped me as I imagined what could have been if I had been there when the burglars had broken in. The sheer shock alone would have probably stopped my heart for sure. That surely was God's mercy on me and Him protecting me.

Most of the things that we'd brought back from the United Kingdom, which were still in boxes at that time, had been stolen. My watch and all my husband's shirts (except those in the washing machine) were taken too. The burglar had used a hand baggage of ours to cart away the goods. I was totally dumbstruck.

We eventually found out that there were two youths involved, one of whom was a young drug addict who lived at the end of the street where I lived, the son of a notable member of the community. My immediate neighbour, an elderly Chinese lady, when interviewed, reported to the police that, apparently, one of them had come disguised as myself, wearing a headdress. She had no idea there was a robbery in progress. They'd feigned arguing with each other, supposedly for not having the key with them. It was their excuse to climb through the back door, which opened out to an open-air backyard within the house. This was a neighbourhood where everyone minded his or her own business, so the Chinese lady did not think too much of what she saw. And at three in the afternoon, the neighbourhood can be a very quiet area to be in. So, I presume the robbers had no difficulties whatsoever in removing their "merchandise".

My husband took me home in the evening to check what else was missing from the house.

Then came the second shock—a major one. The house looked like a war zone. Things were strewn everywhere—clothes, books, and everything else. The shock from the chaos was the final straw and proved too much for me to take in. Something inside me snapped.

As I turned to look at my husband, to my absolute horror, he appeared to me as a two-headed fierce-looking monster with long fangs ready to pounce on me. Red menacing eyes glared at me. It was so horrifyingly shocking that I fell back, cringing in fear. Almost spontaneously, I started to recite the verses from the Holy Quran, hoping to keep my cool and from screaming hysterically.

My husband would surely be scared and think that I might have lost it finally.

Instead, shutting my eyes tightly, I quickly recited the Ayatul Kursi, a verse from the Holy Quran recited for protection against the unseen evil. I was desperately willing the horrifying image to go away. As I continued reciting the verse, I slowly peeped through open slits.

The frightening image was still there, staring at me dangerously.

Thankfully, once again my rational mind took over. I am so truly grateful for my biology lectures during my university days. I'd been taught that, in cases of renal malfunction, when the toxic creatinine rises to a certain level in the blood, it will start to play havoc on the brain. It may cause hallucinations, or the individual might become delusional.

"That's it," I told myself trying to keep calm, while still repeating the holy verse. I quickly concluded that I was at a stage of toxic accumulation in my blood where I was beginning to hallucinate. This piece of knowledge that I'd obtained from my biology class had proven to be very useful and even life-saving. It helped me make sense of what was I was experiencing.

Trying to maintain some composure, I kept on reciting verses from the Holy Quran, greatly comforted in the knowledge that this was just a hallucination due to toxin accumulation. If I did not know otherwise, I would surely have believed I was possessed. Although the fear was very real, both the knowledge and reciting the Quran helped me maintain my composure. The incident further convinced me at that moment that my body was really reaching the limit of toxicity it could tolerate. Slowly, as I calmed down from the continuous recitation of the verses from the Quran, the image finally disappeared.

And so, I am reminded of the words of God in the Holy Quran, pertaining to the importance of knowledge, and how knowledge enlightens the lost soul:

> What about someone who worships devoutly during the night, bowing down, standing in prayer, ever mindful of the life to come, hoping for his Lord's Mercy? Say, "How can those who know be equal to those who do not know?" (The Throngs [Az Zumar] 39: 9–10)

What had happened was that, as my kidneys were failing and they stopped removing the toxic waste materials, my body simply jammed up. It was like having garbage piling up in my own home instead of removing it. Eventually, sooner or later, it started to make me sick. The toxic waste in my body just kept on accumulating and was beginning to cloud my senses and threaten my life—up to a point. Thank God, I still had the sense to realise that, if I did not surrender myself to the hospital soon, I was surely going to die.

Hallucination was not all that I had to bear. I was literally bone skinny until even walking a few steps became a monumental task. My system was so toxic I could not eat without throwing up, and I was even losing control over my bowel movements. That was when I felt I had lost all sense of self-worth. It was time to face reality and take hold of my situation. It was then that my logical brain, the few neurons that were still not affected by the poison, alerted me to how grave and critical my condition really was. To this day, I still cannot believe I could be so stubborn back then—when my whole body was screaming, *Get help!*

Was it fear—fear of facing reality?

And so, two days before the Chinese New Year of 1987, I surrendered myself to the nephrology department. Later, I learned that I was not the only one who'd ever run away. Many other patients had also gone AWOL from their appointments. Some totally disappeared from their families, warranting police searches—at times sadly only too late. Once again, I am most thankful to God for that iota of logical sense still left in me that got me back to the hospital in time.

It was that afternoon when I totally lost control of my bowel movement that I took the decisive move to return to the hospital. I was, at that time, at my parents' house, together with a few brothers and sisters. My siblings never knew the condition I was in at that time of course; all I told them was that I felt it was time I returned to the hospital, as I was not feeling "too good". The old fear of having to be dependent on others was back to haunt me, and it felt real.

"Can any of you guys take me to the hospital? I don't feel too good," I tried to say casually.

"Now? Is there something wrong?" my sister Oni asked. I still remember the concern evident in her voice at that time.

Bless her. Oni had only just returned from Perak, taking care of one of my sisters who was in confinement. Bless my brothers too. They all acted immediately.

I had not planned on getting myself admitted to the hospital, so I finally left with my sister Oni, my husband, and my third brother whom we call Agong. It turned out I was just dressed in my old, worn out baju kurung and 'batik sarong. There wasn't even time to choose a more presentable headdress. Nobody knew how anxious and frightened I was at that time actually. The one-hour drive seemed to drag painfully slowly. I was afraid I would purge in the car. That would be pathetic, not to mention embarrassing.

Once back at the hospital, I was lucky that the nephrology department was willing to let me see the doctor without an appointment. It was a long wait to get to see the doctor—before which I had to have my blood and urine samples taken. Once all the blood tests were done and the results were back, I was steered towards Dr Zaki's room—the unforgettable room 2.

"So, are you done with all your traditional medication? Have you had your fill of coconut juice?"

Ouch! I could still feel the sting as Dr Zaki spoke in his usual gentle voice. That was a sharp give-it-back-to-your-face opening statement from him. And it was not too far from the truth either. I guess I deserved it.

I did not say a word—too tired to argue my defence in a lost cause. I guess Dr Zaki too was used to his patients fleeing appointments only to surrender later. Still, that was as far as he went as his way of reprimanding me, before he was back to his professional self again. He browsed through my blood test results that the nurse had just brought in before he spoke in his deep husky voice.

"The normal level for creatinine in the blood is between 64 to 124 units. Yours is way above that. I am quite surprised that you're still walking about and can still talk reasonably well. You look quite composed," he said, looking straight at me.

I would like to believe that it was my daily practice of reading the Holy Quran that had given me a measure of self-composure and some sense of self-dignity despite the chaos wreaked in my body. All was by the will of God.

Still, I was not about to divulge the truth then and risk getting a serves-you-right remark from him. The truth was that I was so emaciated I couldn't even control my bowel movement.

Dr Zaki turned to my husband and addressed him. "Your wife now has come to a point where the toxic wastes in her blood have reached a critical level that requires dialysis to remove them. But in the long run, a renal transplant would, by far, be the best solution to her condition."

He turned back to look at me before continuing. "A renal transplant would mean that either of your parents or one of your siblings donate one of his or her kidneys to you. An individual can live normally with one functioning kidney," he explained. After a brief pause, he added, "We have discussed this option before, haven't we?" He looked at me.

I nodded and turned to look at my husband.

Some time back, in one of my appointments with Dr Zaki, he had advised me about the possibility of a renal transplant. At that time, he had explained that siblings would make the best donors, since they would share their genetic information coming from the same parents, and therefore, the percentage of compatibility would be higher than with a parent donor.

I had thought about it long and hard back then but had kept it only to myself. I simply did not know how to broach the subject with my family members. And I was also wishing it would not come to this. At that time, apart from my younger sister, all my older brothers and sisters were married and had children to care for. I couldn't possibly make them risk their lives for me.

And now the question stared me in the face again. If I were to have any chance of a normal life again, a renal transplant would be an almost certain solution. I must have looked so serious, thinking how best to bring the matter up with my family.

Dr Zaki seemed to understand my dilemma. He interrupted my worrying thoughts. "Haemodialysis is an option. But there is a long list waiting to get to the very limited number of dialysis machines we have here at the moment. You would have to wait your turn. However, if you're in the renal transplant programme, then we would arrange the necessary procedure to have your transplant performed as early as possible."

That clinched it. I had to try my luck with my family. I had to present my case to them, and hopefully, one of my four brothers and six sisters would be big-hearted enough to come forward.

My chain of thoughts was cut short by Dr Zaki's voice again. "We will admit you into the nephrology ward today and monitor your progress. With the toxin accumulating in your blood now, I feel an immediate dialysis is warranted."

This time, there were no protests from this obstinate person.

It turned out I was admitted for only one night. The Chinese New Year was just around the corner—a long holiday here in Malaysia always. I had come to the hospital only in my baju kurung and batik sarong, with a pair of plain slippers. Given my attire, along with my my gaunt appearance, I guess I must have looked like an ignorant uneducated old woman from a rural village who knew nothing. As such, there ensued a rather awkward incident between the medical officer on call and myself.

I had been admitted just two days before the Chinese New Year, when surely everybody was in the holiday mood, medical officers included. Perhaps he was tired, perhaps he had not quite put on his "doctor cap" yet. But this particular medical officer on call was less than pleased to see me arrive on such a day.

"Couldn't she have come after the holidays? This is such a pain in the ass," he grumbled to the assisting nurse, speaking in English.

Hold on a minute! This medical officer was complaining about me right in front of my face. Didn't he know I could understand him? Then it dawned on me. Perhaps upon seeing my dishevelled appearance, I guess he promptly assumed I could not understand English. To this day, that remains the only explanation I can think of.

His remark rather took me by surprise I must admit. I just looked up and stared blankly—no animosity, no anger, just fatigue and perhaps with a little bit of regret that a medical officer should judge a book by its cover. Giving him the benefit of a doubt, I told myself he was probably having a bad hair day.

The next day happened to be the grand round day, when the specialists made their rounds to meet patients and be briefed by the medical officer with regards to the patients' progress. When they came to me, Dato Abu Bakar immediately said smilingly, "Hey, Prohoeman, it's your niece, the Salford girl."

After a brief exchange of greetings with my uncle and answering a few questions asked by Dr Bakar, the latter suddenly asked if I wanted to go home.

Of course I did. Could I?

"I think we can allow you to be with your family this holiday season, provided you can come back here immediately if you feel worse. Do you think you can do that?"

Certainly I could. A new appointment was soon scheduled for me to come back again the following week to start my dialysis.

All throughout my conversation with Dr Bakar and my uncle, both of whom spoke only in English with me, I could see from the corner of my eye the medical officer staring at me and looking distinctly uncomfortable. Perhaps he was trying to recall what he had said about me to the nurse the previous day. He was a young man, possibly around my age at that time, and just for a moment then, I felt like teasing him into further discomfort. I turned to look at him and gave him the I-know-what-you-said-yesterday smile. His eyes momentarily grew wide before he looked down hurriedly at the notes he had in his hands. That was a sweet moment of triumph for me. Today I can only hope that the medical officer learnt something from this experience—never to judge a book by its cover. Everyone needs to be kind, especially doctors.

In the end, I was sent back home again, with my handful of medication, awaiting dialysis. I knew that this was the time for me to approach my family about donating a kidney.

It was a quiet Chinese New Year holiday, as far as everyone else was concerned; but it was a heavy load I carried on my shoulders. How was I going to ask any of my siblings for a kidney, which involved surgery, when all my older sisters and brothers were married and had families of their own? Being the second youngest from a family of eleven, my father and mother were forty-six and thirty-six respectively when they had me, so when I was twenty-six, a simple calculation would show that my parents were just too old for me to ask for something as taxing to their health as a kidney donation.

I finally decided the best way to approach the issue was to go directly into the heart of the matter. A family gathering arranged by my father gave me the opportunity I needed.

"The doctors said that my kidneys have deteriorated and that I will have to start dialysis after the Chinese New Year. But Dr Zaki said that my only chance of a cure would be a renal transplant—from one of my siblings."

There! That was it; I had said what needed to be said.

Silence immediately ensued. There was some shuffling of the feet, and almost everyone showed anxious faces. I can totally understand their reactions. To give up an organ from inside you for someone else, even your own kith and kin demanded the greatest sacrifice and a certain risk to your health. It would be different if it were for your own children. Parents would die for their children. I held my breath, waiting for someone to speak up.

I must have been blessed for reasons I know not why. For despite all the doubts and hesitancy, not to mention the risks, not one but two of my siblings stepped up to volunteer as a donor. My fifth sister, Oni, spoke first.

"As you all probably know, my sister-in-law is a renal failure patient, and she is on dialysis now. I have seen her condition, and I know what it is like to live as a renal failure patient. I don't mind giving you one of my kidneys, sis."

The other was my third brother, Agong as he is known among us.

"I wouldn't mind being tested for eligibility," he said.

The former was thirty-two at that time, whilst the latter was thirty. Let me share something about these two wonderful persons in my life.

Oni is the seventh in my family. She is rather plump; hence nieces and nephews call her "Mak Mok" (chubby aunt). She has tan skin and stands just over five feet tall. But what is distinct about her is her jovial nature and friendliness. It's always easy to strike up a conversation with Oni. She's married with three beautiful daughters, and her husband was a worker at the Port Klang Authorities, handling the heavy machinery loading and unloading cargo. Oni's sister-in-law was a renal failure patient herself and had been on dialysis for quite a long time. She has since passed away; God bless her soul. She did not have a donor and was on the list for cadaveric donor. When she was in her critical stage of ESRD, without any hope of a new kidney, it was my sister who travelled back and forth taking care of her and attending to her needs. My sister Oni is simply that kind of a person—first to offer help to those in need. She is a woman with a bubbly nature who simply likes to help others. She did it out of compassion that was in her, not expecting any rewards or praise. At one point, she even told her sister-in-law that, should such calamity befall her own siblings, she would not hesitate to come forward to donate one of her kidneys.

She would tell me later that God had tested her for the sincerity of her words—through me.

"When you said you needed a kidney, I was immediately reminded of the words I'd once told my sister-in-law. So now I am fulfilling my words to God," she had explained.

Not only did Oni volunteer to donate her kidney, but throughout my hospitalisation days, she was also my staunch supporter, my source of strength, leaving her family during the weekends to take care of me in hospital. I would not have had the strength to continue if not for her unyielding support, her constant companionship, and just simply her presence. She was indeed my pillar of strength.

Then there was my big brother Agong, who is the eighth in the family. He was dark like me but much taller. He was a personnel officer and had a keen interest and concern for the welfare of others. We were very close as children; he was always upfront in lending a hand. In my family, since the both of us were the ones who had darker complexion, naturally we were very close. In fact, my big brother Agong is a person that is easily loved by all, children especially. I believe being close to me, he was quick to volunteer as a donor.

What can a little sister who is desperate for a kidney say when not one but two of her siblings step forward to donate their kidney? God is surely Great. We had a father who kept the family unit together all his life and who was exemplary in showing the importance of the family unit staying together. We had a mother who, in so many ways, was different from my strict father. Where Abah was strict, Mak was more jovial but very protective whenever the situation called for it. Mak would readily dance to a happy tune and sang songs like "Moonlight and Shadows". Yet if she ever found out that her children were being ridiculed by some bullying young men in the neighbourhood (as happened once to my big brother Agong and I when we were still in school), you would find her confronting the biggest of them, her sleeves pulled back, ready to fight for her children's sake.

That combination was what that blessed me with sisters and brothers who had compassion for others and big enough hearts to withstand physical barriers when challenged.

To this very day, I cannot praise God enough, nor thank my brother and sister for coming forward sufficiently. Even if, in the end, the outcome had not been what I'd hoped for, I can never describe the gratitude I feel at their willingness to come forward for the sake of their little sister—for no other reason but simply their love for me. Their coming forward as volunteers gave me the strength and hope that things would somehow turn out all right in the end.

And if I have failed to say this enough times, I will say it one more time, time and again—thank you from the bottom of my heart, and I love you guys to no end. All praise to God.

In the meantime, I just had to hang on.

God has spoken in the Holy Quran:

> Faint not nor grieve, for ye will overcome them
> if ye are (indeed) believers. (the Family of 'Imran
> [AliImran] 3:139)

CHAPTER

9

IPD

You never know how
strong
You are
Until being strong is the
only
Choice you have

This was the beginning of a journey in my life that would be the most sobering, most humbling and most torturous—a part which I would gladly leave forgotten. Yet, through the pain, the ordeal, I shall only say this—what did not kill me only made me stronger.

And wiser, I hope.

It was a Friday afternoon that marked the beginning of my tour of dialysis. Prior to that, I had gone to see Dr Zaki with both my brother and sister as potential donors. Immediately, blood tests were done to ascertain who among them had the same blood group as mine. Both turned out compatible to mine—A+. However before further tests could be carried out, I found out that my brother's wife was a bit reluctant to have her husband be in the donor list. I could understand her apprehensiveness. He was the head of the family, the breadwinner. Perhaps she was worried that things might go wrong with the surgery or afterwards.

I can totally relate to what my sister-in-law must have beenthinking. They had only just had a baby boy; she would surely need her husband around. It would be difficult to care for a recuperating husband as well as an infant at the same time. It was not fair for me to take his time away from his wife and young son.

That left my hope only with my sister Oni. I was praying hard. I knew she was sincere in wanting to donate one of her kidneys to me. I just wasn't sure what her husband was thinking. I know a lot of the worries at that time came from the lack of information on the renal transplant itself.

Actually, even back then, Malaysia was already ahead of its time in renal transplant surgery, spearheaded by Dr Hussein Awang—with more than ten years of experience in renal transplant at that time. Still, to me, it was imperative that anyone who was to be my donor should want to donate his or her kidney full-heartedly.

But that was not enough. Both my potential donors had families. It was equally important, for my peace of mind if nothing else, that their spouses were okay with them being donors—that there would not be any repercussions later. Thankfully, Oni was still sure about donating one of her kidneys, and so it was decided that she would proceed with further tests to determine the percentage of compatibility between her kidney and mine as far as kidney structure was concerned.

And so, it came to be that on that particular Friday, in the afternoon, my sister arrived from Klang where I was staying in Petaling Jaya to accompany me for my hospital admission. It was just the two of us. Neither of us knew how to drive at that time; nor did we have any personal mode of transportation. We took a taxi from Petaling Jaya to Kuala Lumpur Hospital (HKL) and headed straight to Ward 4A of the nephrology department. Not only was my sister Oni willing to donate her kidney, but she had also volunteered to keep me company for my hospital stay.

"During dialysis, you'll need someone to attend to you when you are bedridden, trust me," she had said. She must have known this from the days when she'd taken care of her sister-in-law.

When I'd ditched my hospital appointment the previous year, I had revoked my chance to have a fistula done to enable me to start my haemodialysis programme. A fistula is an enlarged vein, usually positioned in the arm, which is created by connecting an artery directly to a vein. This creates a much greater blood flow into the vein as is required during haemodialysis. As a result, the vein enlarges and strengthens, making insertion of needles for haemodialysis treatments easier. Since I'd failed to show up to have the fistula procedure done, alternative measures had to be considered for patients in urgent need of dialysis.

Without the fistula, the alternative left for me was to undergo intermittent peritoneal dialysis. In intermittent peritoneal dialysis, or IPD, as it was referred to by my fellow ESRD patients, the peritoneum in the abdomen is used as a membrane across which fluids and dissolved substances are exchanged from the blood. I was informed about it without fully understanding what it meant or what it would do to me. I did not have the faintest idea that what I was about to experience would turn out to be the most trying and most painful trial in my life thus far. Had I known what I had to endure by going through the peritoneal dialysis, I would most certainly not have played truant during one of the most important appointments of my life. I would have had the fistula created on my arm, which would surely have spared me a terrible ordeal. That certainly was a lesson learnt the hard way for me.

When I arrived at the ward, I saw several patients with tubes attached at one end to a bag of fluid hanging onto an IV stand and the other end disappearing somewhere around their abdomens. Renal failure patients were plentiful then, so there was no hope of getting into first class, which I was eligible for.

Later I was told that the hospital administration was keener to have peritoneal dialysis patients placed in the third-class ward, all grouped together in one place, where they could be more closely observed. In a way, I was glad I was placed there, rather than being alone in a first-class room when I was bedridden during those times I was on IPD. Having to wear my headdress all the time was just a small inconvenience. However, for my sister's sake—she had to sacrifice, sleeping on the lounge chair and bearing with all forms of discomfort—I requested a first-class meal that hopefully would make up a bit for the hardship and discomfort she had to suffer for my sake. My request was approved; the nurses were grateful whenever dialysis patients had family members helping out in their care at the hospital.

I remember asking one of the patients next to me if the procedure was painful. Although she was dark, you could see that her face was pale, with dry lips, a tell-tale sign of renal failure patients. But what I won't forget was the way she smiled knowingly at me and how she answered my question very diplomatically and philosophically.

"It's a different personal experience with every patient. But hey, don't worry," she said, and I do remember till today the almost sympathetic look she gave me. (I wonder where she is now; we lost contact over the years.)

Somehow, her "hey, don't worry" only got me more anxious. In no time at all, a young female doctor approached me. We talked for a while; she asked me a few questions, and I answered her as best I could. Then she finally asked me if I knew what I had come in for. I told her I had come for dialysis, not forgetting to let her know that I wasn't at all clear what it meant. So, the kind doctor went on to explain what it was that she was about to do to me.

A PD catheter (Tenckhoff catheter) was to be inserted into my abdomen, as I had no fistula to enable me to perform haemodialysis. In haemodialysis, the cleansing fluid would be injected into my blood system. However, for peritoneal dialysis, the cleansing fluid would be injected into the peritoneal space in my abdomen, where, through the process of diffusion, wastes from my blood would enter the dialysis solution, whilst the necessary salts required by my body would diffuse from the dialysis fluid into my body system. The fluid would be left to dwell in my body for four to five hours to ensure maximum cleansing and removal of toxic wastes before it was drained out and replaced with a new bag of dialysis solution, and the whole process would begin again.

Well ... okay ... I could grasp the mechanics of the whole procedure. Only one question now remained in my mind.

How was the catheter to be inserted into my peritoneum?

Anxiously I awaited the answer as the doctor slowly explained the procedure.

A small slit would be made somewhere on my abdomen just under my navel, taking special care not to cut a blood vessel. I would be given local anaesthetics of course. Then the catheter would be inserted through the slit on my skin and pushed gently in right until it reached the peritoneal cavity. I would remain bedridden from then till Sunday, when the catheter will be removed, the slit closed up, and I could go back to my daily business at home and workplace.

This was one time when I thought it was better to simply be ignorant and to just take things as they came. But oh no! My brain was exploding with questions.

Wait a minute. I noted I'll be given local anaesthetics, but that will only be on my skin; it will only be skin deep, won't it? What happens when she pushes the catheter right until it reaches my peritoneal cavity? My head was screaming with furious frightened alert sirens.

It wasn't long before I discovered the answer for myself.

The procedure was done on the hospital bed where I was placed in the ward. My sister was kindly asked to leave the premises, and the green curtains were pulled around my bed to isolate me from the other patients. It was just the doctor, the dialysis paraphernalia, and me.

The local anaesthesia was applied. After a transient pain when she inserted the needle and shot in the anaesthetics, the skin on my abdomen was soon numb to any sensations and I did not even notice when the slit was made on my skin right below my navel. When the doctor pulled out the catheter, I looked away. I knew how a catheter looked from previous hospital admissions, and I did not want my courage to run out on me at that crucial moment. She told me to relax, as she was about to insert the catheter through the slit she had just made.

At first, I felt no pain as the catheter slid into the slit. But the next thing I knew I was suddenly being stabbed alive! The pain was excruciating; inch by torturous inch, I could feel the catheter slowly slicing through my muscles as it made its way down the slit. My urge was to double over, and I desperately tried to push the doctor's hands off me. Where was the anaesthesia that was supposed to be working to numb my pain? I cried for the torture to stop, willing the doctor to stop as the tears automatically spilled down my face; it was just unbearable. But only whimpers escaped my lips.

"Doctor, it hurts … it hurts," was all I could murmur. Immediately, the doctor told me to relax (as if that were possible), take deep breaths, and not harden my abdominal muscles. Contracting the muscles would only worsen the situation and make it harder to push the catheter further into the body. The doctor was a small lady, and I could see her hands shaking as she struggled to push the catheter through the layers of muscles on my abdomen. Being extremely thin, I assure you, there were not many layers of muscles and hardly any fat anywhere on my body.

I tried my best to relax and to take deep breaths but found it almost impossible when I realised that I was literally being stabbed as the lady doctor continued pushing the catheter inside me. Oh, God, please let it end; death would be a blessed relief. I cried inwardly, and that was when I remembered, just like I had a few years ago during the biopsy in the United Kingdom, that only invoking God's name would bring me peace again, albeit momentarily. I drew in a deep breath and started invoking God's name reminding myself of the words of Prophet Muhammad (peace be upon him):

> Nothing afflicts a Muslim of hardship, nor illness, nor anxiety, nor sorrow, nor harm, nor distress, nor even the pricking of a thorn, but that Allah will expiate his sins by it. (Bukhari and Muslim)

I could only pray God was taking a hefty chunk of sins off me.

That brought some comfort in a skewed kind of way and a little strength to bear what I was being subjected to.

This is a test of patience from God. God knows that I can withstand this. He is testing me. Help me pull this through, Allah, I tried to comfort myself.

Gradually, I became less agitated, and I remember the look of relief on the poor doctor's face as I calmed down. After what seemed like a very long time, it was finally over. I was now hooked on to the dialysis bag on the IV stand. My dialysis had begun.

I take this memory with me for always. In retrospect, I cannot deny that the procedure was painful. It hurt very much, but I made it. The worst moment was over, and I got to continue with my life. To me, that was the most important thing; it helped me survive that bit longer. The doctor had to do what she had to do. She was not the enemy here. It was unfortunate that my kidneys failed me. It was unfortunate that I had to go through this pain, but I lived. Running away is not a solution; it's just a tragedy. Such is life—there will be pain at one point or another in our lives. But to give up and to run away before even giving the self a chance to fight is just admitting defeat. And that is sad while there is still a chance. We just need to find the strength within; and the one source of strength lies with God surely. I was still young; there was a lot waiting for me in the future. I'd survived the loss of my firstborn son; I should not let his sacrifice go in vain. I often think his untimely demise was his sacrifice so I could live. I must honour that sacrifice by fighting to stay above all these trials.

Realising all this, I let the tears flow. It was my way of cradling my pain, nursing my wound, and washing away my hurt so I could move on.

When the curtains were pulled back and the doctor left me, my sister rushed to my side, and I broke down. As she gently rubbed my arms in comfort, only God knew how grateful I was to have her by my side at that moment. She stroked my head in a way that told me she sympathised without even saying a word; she just let me cry.

Later I looked at the patient next to me who I had talked to earlier, and she smiled quietly back at me. I finally understood and returned her smile feebly. There was no way she could have described this to me. It was something I had to experience myself to understand. I had just gone through what must be the most harrowing experience in my life. To this day, I would tell anyone whenever I am asked about intermittent peritoneal dialysis, it is something I would never wish to happen to even my worst enemy, if I had one. And I prayed that no other renal failure patients would ever have to go through this. I vowed I would never go AWOL on my appointments from then on; this was such a high price to pay for my truancy.

The tube that was attached to my abdomen had a tap where the used fluid would be drained periodically and new fresh dialysis solution brought in. My abdomen felt sore, and it hurt. And because I had gas problems, the pain was aggravated, and I would groan in agony. Later I learnt from other patients that the IPD would be less painful if I didn't have so much gas in my abdomen. I was quick to remember that.

Later in the evening when the reality of my fate started to sink in, and I was more settled emotionally, I remember my sister asking me how it felt.

My answer? "Now I know what it is like to be stabbed alive."

What I had just gone through was intermittent peritoneal dialysis, where my system was being cleansed transitorily. From Friday through to Sunday, I was bedridden, my abdomen too sore to sit up for any length of time. When I needed to urinate, my sister would place the bedpan beneath my bottom. When

I was done, I would clean myself up as best I could before Oni removed it from my bed. She kept a vigilant watch over me, just stroking my arm whenever she saw me wince. She fussed over me and made jokes to distract my mind from my situation.

She was my Mother Teresa.

She was my fortress of strength.

She was there for me—a big sister, a nurse, and a companion.

For all that time, never once did I see any signs of regret or revulsion as she removed my excretory wastes. Throughout the three days, she was beside me when I was awake, and she was beside me when I was asleep. The nurses would come over and make light talk with her; Oni was an easy person to warm up to. She always had this jovial smiling face on her.

On Sunday afternoon, the dialysis was stopped, and I had to go through another ordeal to have the catheter removed from inside me. Again, I cried out when the same doctor pulled out the catheter—as gently as she could, I was sure. Again, I was told to take deep breaths and relax. Relax? Ironic really, since in that moment of intense pain, all I could do was gasp. In fact, I could hardly breathe from the sheer pain. The doctor then patched up the slit; it turned out, thankfully, no stitches were required. She examined me a while, ordered blood tests to be taken, and declared me fit enough to be discharged—only with the reminder to come back again the following Friday, to go through all this once again … and again … and again. God have mercy.

Every Friday became a day of anxiety and dread for me. I would be filled with angst, knowing I had to go through the procedure when I walked into the hospital ward and have myself hooked to a tube for three days until Sunday. My only consolation, and strength really, was that my sister would always be with me for all the three days when I would be immobile and bedridden.

I would head straight to the third-class quarters of Ward 4A and report to the nurse, who would assign me a bed. Then I would make small talk with the other patients already hooked on to the tube. After coming in for dialysis and going through this routine week after week, one simply got used to the other patients who, like me, came back for their weekly IPD too. We even began to get familiar with the nurses and vice versa.

One patient was a recent school leaver, a young Malay girl who never had anyone to visit her each time she came in for dialysis. Initially, she was aloof and apparently unfriendly. But I, being a teacher, and my sister a mother, we could understand her seeming couldn't-care-less attitude. It was just a front. We felt it was her defence against the world, so to speak. Being a teacher to young teenagers, I felt strongly that she was just trying to show us that she did not need anyone—simply because no one actually came to visit. Each time her brother would just deposit her at the hospital bed and leave.

I was well tended to by my sister, and I had everything I needed each time I went to the ward—my books, my drinks, and my snacks; the necessary utensils; and, most of all, my big sister. Most of the time, Oni would be with me just entertaining me with small talk when I was awake. Being a very compassionate person, she would take pity on the poor girl and go over to talk to her.

In the beginning the young girl appeared to be quite stand-offish, but my sister's motherly nature soon won her over. Since she had nothing with her, not even a spoon, my sister would make her hot drinks, make sure she took her medicines, clean her up, and simply fuss over her like a mother would while she lay bedridden on IPD. I was worried my sister would tire herself out from taking care of the both of us, but I need not have worried. My sister did whatever she did out of her natural caring self and did not mind. So I let her.

In no time, the young girl became my sister's adopted "ward". And every time we walked into the ward for dialysis over the weekend, anyone could see the obvious relief in her eyes to see my sister in particular. Later I learnt that the young girl had requested that she be admitted at the same time my sister and I were hospitalised and even asked to be in the same part of the hospital ward with us.

Then there was this other girl, a young Chinese lady about my age at that time. She too had no one to visit her, except for an ailing mother who stayed with her in the ward to care for her. She did not talk much, preferring to listen to other people talk— probably because she could not talk Malay much. I admired her; she was cool in almost any situation. When in pain, she would only whimper and sigh. When she was feeling cheerful, she would just smile quietly, almost expressionless. Occasionally, my sister would also tend to her just to give some moments of relief to the poor ailing mother.

Sadly, both these girls had no plans for a renal transplant. My Chinese friend had only her mother, who was too old to donate a kidney. As for the young girl, it was a pity that her family members did not even turn up to visit her, let alone volunteer to be a kidney donor. She went on for a few more peritoneal dialyses, and then one day, she just disappeared. My sister got concerned and asked the nurses about the poor little girl. The reply was so sad. One of the nurses informed her that the youngster had become upset that her family members were not supportive, and so she just decided one day not to turn up for dialysis anymore. My sister was upset; I knew she would gladly have taken care of the young girl, and it would not be too much of a burden to her. God knows the poor young girl would not have survived more than a fortnight without dialysis. We never heard from her again after that.

As for Oni, whenever she could not come to take care of me over the weekend, my younger sister, Lili, would come in her place to take care of me. One thing about Lili though, as she is my younger sister, I often felt responsible for her. I always felt at odds having her take care of me instead. So, during her shift to look after me, I would try my best to put up a stronger front, and I would make a real effort to talk to her whenever I could. I tried to keep her company at the same time.

Unfortunately for Lili, the few times she came to take care of me, there would be a death in the ward each time—usually in the middle of the night. The hospital attendants would come with the trolley, its clanking sounding louder than usual in the silence of the night. This would inevitably wake my younger sister, and she would watch wide-eyed to see death at such close range. However, one good thing about Lili, who was still single at that time; she would always find a way to make light of things. Ultimately, she and I would end up giggling over something even during trying or sobering moments. May God forgive us.

At other times, whenever Oni needed to leave the hospital for short periods of time to get something in town, my cousin, the late Kak Melah would come and sit in with me. Kak Melah was a friendly person in her own right, but I guess she never had any common topics to talk with me about, as she was quite a bit older than me. Still, her porridge was out of this world. I was so blessed that my family really cared for me in my hours of need. It is my belief that all of them never minded sitting in for my sister Oni because they all genuinely wanted to give Oni a break, considering her compassion and tenacity in taking care of me at the hospital. Not many people can do what Oni did, sacrificing part of her life like she did.

All this was way back in 1987. Haemodialysis machines were few and very limited then. It was a long wait to get to the haemodialysis machine. I just had to endure the weekly intermittent peritoneal dialysis in the hospital. I was lucky to be a schoolteacher, for I got the weekend free to get myself admitted into the hospital, when other people worked the six-day week at that time.

I was lucky in other ways too. I had a very supportive family. Each visiting hour, someone from my family would visit me and give a moment of reprieve for my sister Oni. My sister was always with me, making my stay at the hospital bearable. I did not talk much when I was sick, so my sister would be filling me in on information she gained from the nurses who she'd befriended and from other fellow patients. She was friendly to all—beloved Kak Oni to all the patients in the wing of the hospital ward where I was placed.

One thing I must really thank God for is that my family members were educated enough to be open-minded. They were not opposed to the idea of an organ transplant. Most people back then were wary and uneasy about organ donation; reciting religion as an excuse that one should not die with parts of their body missing (which is false, by the way). Some were just ignorant and making up stories, saying that they had very "thick blood" that was just not suitable for organ donations. Religious scepticism and ignorance were the main excuses. As far as I could tell, I think it was mainly just fear that made those people say all those things.

When one volunteers to be an organ donor, extensive and stringent tests are carried out before he or she can qualify as a donor. The aged are not encouraged to be donors. Many factors—physical, emotional, and clinical aspects must be looked into first.

In Islam, organ transplant is allowed. So, the refusal to become a donor based on religion is simply not acceptable. For the Chinese, many said back then that to donate part of one's body is bad luck. But I dare say that the Chinese community now are educated enough not to use such excuses for not donating an organ. Today, patients who cannot get a living related donor might opt to "purchase" a kidney from India initially and, more recently, Taiwan. Most Chinese patients practice this. There are also people who have signed up to have their organs donated upon their death. Renal transplant from these non-related donors and cadaveric donors pose a higher risk of rejection than transplants from living related donors. However, presently there are various medications to minimise this risk of rejection.

The only thing that can halt an organ transplant is that the donor must do so voluntarily. The donor himself or herself must be willing to donate one of his or her organs. We patients know this, and we do know that what we're asking for is a lot. However, in no way are we forcing anyone to take any risks. There is no need to patronise us with lame excuses. It is not helpful to our state of minds. Fate has it that, somehow, we are the ones whom God has chosen to be tested with renal failure. For most of us, we accept this fate, and we do our very best to make the best of the situation we're in. So, if no help can be given, there's no need to give any reasons or excuses. It will be painful for us to accept that reality. But rest assured, we can truly understand.

The other thing was that, during my stay in the hospital, being confined to my bed for almost seventy-two hours, it was almost impossible for me to perform the proper rituals of *solat*, the five daily prayers for Muslims. But perform them I must, as that is the decree from God, in any moment and situation I am in:

> Such as remember Allah, standing, sitting, and reclining, and consider the creation of the heavens and the earth, (and say): Our Lord! Thou created not this in vain. Glory be to Thee!

Preserve us from the doom of Fire. (The family
of 'Imran [Ali 'Imran] 3:191)

So, I tried to do to the best I could, given the state I was
in. Without my sister I could not perform the *istinja* (cleansing)
properly with water for my ablution. Still, if I were on my own,
my ablution would be performed with the dry method—without
water but by using dust instead—the *tayamum,* as is decreed in
the Holy Quran:

> O ye who believe! When ye rise up for prayer,
> wash your faces, and your hands up to the
> elbows, and lightly rub your heads and (wash)
> your feet up to the ankles. And if ye are unclean,
> purify yourselves, And if ye are sick or on a
> journey, or one of you cometh from the closet,
> or ye have had contact with women, and ye find
> not water, then go to clean, high ground and
> rub your faces and your hands with some of it.
> Allah would not place a burden on you, but He
> would purify you and would perfect His grace
> upon you, that ye may give thanks. (The Feast
> [Al Maidah] 5:6)

And I would pray whilst lying on my back, for praying is
ordained at its appointed time, even if it means just by signalling
with movements of our eyes.

Thus, it is a sad thing for me to recall my other friends not
performing the prayers throughout their stay during dialysis.
Some gave the excuse that they did not feel clean; others said
they felt awkward praying while lying down.

Being a Muslim, I believe my religion is not one that imposes
hard rules on its followers. The time of solat is a time specifically
allocated to the remembrance of God. What is important is that

we perform the rituals and leave the rest to His judgement. To take up the spirit of prayer itself and to respect and observe the prayer times—that's what matters in our difficult times during dialysis. We are taught by the words of our beloved prophet (peace be upon him) that when we are ill, God is with us (Bukhari). Therefore, it is all the more meaningful for us to connect with Him during this time. Basically, I do not blame my fellow patients; nor am I judging them. At that time and age, not many people were exposed to and truly understood Islam as it should be practiced. I am glad now that more and more people are being exposed to the true nature and spirit of Islam—that it is not merely a religion of strict rituals that must be followed blindly but that Islam is a religion of mercy; it is the religion of connecting oneself to God, to His remembrance in the best way we can. The rituals are there as a guideline but there is always room for emergencies, as in the tayamum.

I can only pray and hope that Muslim patients today don't take lightly this matter of prayer or solat and connecting with Him even in the direst straits. We need Him, especially in our moments of trials and tribulations, and He understands the predicament we are in. He is all knowing. He is always there beside us; all we need to do is seek Him out—in any way we can. He understands. Who else would know how to fix us if not He who has created us?

> [Prophet], if My servants ask you about Me,
> I am near. I respond to those who call Me, so
> let them respond to Me, and believe in Me, so
> that they may be rightly guided. (The Cow [Al
> Baqarah] 2:186]

My own personal relationship with God was built in this way. In all those days when I was afflicted with ESRD, the solat, praying to God, were the moments that gave me peace and temporary relief from my illness, my troubles, and my fears. Those were my downtime moments with God—where I would pour out my most private feelings to Him. And I would feel a sense of comfort and solace after venting out my emotions to Him, the One God, who knows all our secrets in the deepest recesses of our hearts. Prayers brought about patience in me—the patience to endure what fate had thrown on my path of life. This sense of peace was not something tangible, but it was something I felt strongly in my heart and soul, and that was the factor that gave me strength to persevere. I knew God was with me:

> You who believe, seek help through steadfastness and prayer, for God is with the steadfast. (The Cow [Al Baqarah] 2:153)

CHAPTER

10

—

Laughter and Tears

Strength of character isn't always about how much you can handle before you break; it's also about how much you can handle after you're broken.

"The ship is sinking. Water is coming in from all directions. We have to abandon ship now. I am getting soaked. It's cold. I must get out of here. But I can't move. There's something tying me down. Help!"

I struggled to free myself and started turning and tossing till I finally woke up with a start. For a moment, I was puzzled, bewildered, and unsure where I was. I looked around me, feeling very cold … and very wet. It was just a dream. But why was the soaking real?

I checked and saw the tube jutting out from my abdomen, fluid steadily seeping from the gap on my abdomen. I followed the path of the tube up to the almost empty dialysis bag hanging on the hook stand beside my bed. Slowly, realisation hit me. I was on my hospital bed undergoing my IPD, only instead of the dialysis solution coming into my abdomen, it was leaking out through my abdomen, leaving me soaked to the bone in a pool of dialysis fluid on the mattress.

I looked at my watch beside me; it was 2.30 in the morning. Turning around in my flooded bed, I saw my sister fast asleep on the lounging chair. With shaking fingers and chattering teeth, I reached out to her and struggled to wake her up.

"Oni, Oni, wake up. I am drowning in this bed."

My sister was immediately wide-awake and stared blankly at me—a shocked and confused look in her eyes.

"Where is all this water coming from, sis?"

"It's the dialysis fluid. It's leaking from my abdomen. Get the nurse, please. I am shivering here," I said. It was difficult to speak, with my teeth chattering uncontrollably.

Oni rushed to alert the night nurse. And when she arrived, she too stared at the pitiful state I was in. Shaking her head in disbelief, she suggested that perhaps the slit on my abdomen was a wee bit too large this time, and my movements might perhaps have loosened the position of the catheter, further causing the dialysis fluid to leak through the gap on my abdomen.

"I'm afraid we may have to remove the catheter first, Fizah, and get the doctor to re-insert a new one. I will get the doctor to see you later."

Bummer! Just my luck to be drowned in my own dialysis solution. And later I would have to go through yet another stabbing. Talk about things going terribly wrong.

The tube was quickly and easily removed, not surprisingly, and the gap on my abdomen temporarily covered with bandage and plaster. My sister then led me to the toilet to change into dry clothes. When I returned to my bed, the mattress had been changed, with a dry warm one waiting for me—thank the Most Merciful God. However, I was puzzled by my sister's hearty laugh. I wondered what was so amusing to her at three o'clock in the morning.

"Why are you laughing? What's so funny?" I asked, perplexed.

"You are! You should see how you looked all drenched on the bed just now, surrounded by water. You looked like a drowned rat. And the way you were walking, you looked just like an old frail lady, the way you were staggering to the toilet, your wet clothes trailing. I'm sorry, but you were truly in a sorry state that it just looked so funny. You poor, poor girl."

I simply had to agree. I could see myself dragging my feet and shivering uncontrollably as I made my way to the toilet earlier. My teeth could not stop chattering. I must have looked a sight.

I remember after that both of us laughing our way into the wee hours of the morning as I relayed to my sister my dream and the hilarity of the situation—and the shock on my sister's face to find me drowning in my own bed, my arms flailing in desperate attempt to stay afloat.

One thing I can say now is this, I thank God Almighty that, although He had put me through this trial of being terminally ill at that time, He had not taken away my sense of humour. I am so thankful I could still find the humour in my desperate situation, and I'm grateful to my sister for making light of the mess I was in. I felt rejuvenated for a moment in time. Looking at the incident from the comical point of view made what I was going through bearable. For a moment I forgot I was an end-stage renal disease patient—a terminally ill patient dependent on dialysis to continue living. I was back to just being my old self again, just a simple ordinary servant of God, having a "goof-up" moment.

Alhamdulillah ala kulli hal - All praise be to God in all circumstances.

Not all the jokes were on me, however. Once, in the middle of the night, the night nurse came to change my dialysis bag. It was again around two in the morning (a good time for dreaming I suppose). On that particular night, the nurse was wearing a gown that was up to her knees (not the usual blouse and pants that most nurses wore). And as she approached me, she had to go over my sister, who was sleeping on the lounge chair next to my bed. The lounge chair was reclined so my sister was, in fact, lying lower down. Deftly avoiding the chair in her effort not to wake my sister up, the nurse was lifting her arms to take out the used dialysis bag from the hook on the stand. All the time she was doing this, her skirt would float over my sister's face, occasionally brushing her nose.

Now, my sister Oni was and still is asthmatic and, needless to say, has a very sensitive nose. As the nurse's skirt rode over her nose, absently, in her sleep, my sister would push the hem of the skirt away from her face. Sensing something amusing was about to follow, I watched in fascinated anticipation the subtle play between the two ladies. When my sister brushed the hem of the skirt away from her face in her slumber, inevitably her hand would go up the nurse's legs above the knee. This must have been most uncomfortable for the nurse, so she had to use one hand to push away my sister's fumbling fingers. This distracted her from the task of changing my dialysis bag. The silent tête-à-tête between nurse and big sister was bringing the laughter bubbling inside me. I could not help the chuckle that escaped my lips.

The final straw came when, as the nurse reached up high to hook up the new bag of dialysis fluid, her skirt hem brushed fully over my sister's whole face. I do not know what dream my sister was having for she suddenly pushed her hand right up into the nurse's skirt to push it off her face. The nurse jumped and gave a loud yelp in utter shock; my sister woke up, startled. I burst out laughing.

Oni, who was still half asleep, sat up with a lost and confused look on her face. The nurse stared at her with flushed face, not speaking at all, giving my sister a deathly stare. I wouldn't be surprised if she thought my sister had a maniacal streak in her. I could not help laughing watching the two of them.

Indeed, laughter is the best medicine. My pain momentarily forgotten, I took my turn to have a good laugh at my sister as I listened to her recounting the dream that was surely connected to the incident.

There was also one time when we both cheated on the nurses. During IPD, the dialysis fluid would be brought into my abdomen gradually over a period of time. It would take several hours to allow all the fluid to flow into my abdomen. This could be quite frustrating at times, especially when, at that time, we thought that the faster the dialysis solution bags were exchanged, the faster we could go home.

So, once Oni and I decided to speed things up a bit. When the nurses were not looking, she would turn on the tap to the tube a bit wider to allow more of the dialysis solution to flow in. That way, we were hoping the removal would be hastened too. Those times the nurses were rather puzzled why I was filling up much faster than the other patients.

"Did anyone touch this?" the nurse on duty would ask my sister.

"No, nobody," my sister would answer innocently with her poker face.

And I would shake my head profusely—the perfect accomplice.

When the nurse left, we would both be giggling away, feeling triumphant.

All that was until I learnt that the slow inflow was to ensure that as much toxic waste was removed from my body and the proper timing was actually crucial to the effectiveness of the IPD session.

When we learnt about it, guilt crept in, and we never cheated again.

At other times, the source of laughter came from the other patients. One patient, who was in hospital for dialysis the same days I was in, was a frail elderly Chinese lady who did not have anyone to care for her. She had lost most of her hair. (I found out later that renal failure could do this to patients. I am glad this did not happen to me.) Unfortunately, it was against both our interests whenever we were placed beside each other in the ward.

She could not stand the cold, and I was always feeling heaty.

One night, I was feeling extraordinarily hot and humid and was finding it difficult to sleep. Oni noticed my restlessness and went over to switch on the fan to cool us off. As it happened, on that occasion this particular lady was placed beside my bed. As soon as the fan was spinning, she started to grumble that it was too cold. She got off her bed, slowly staggered towards the switch to turn it off, and then stumbled back to her bed.

"Oni, why is it hot again?" I cried out to my sister. Patiently, Oni got up to switch the fan on again. And once again, the Chinese lady, grudgingly got off her bed to switch it off. My sister then got up again when I started to complain about the heat.

Eventually, the Chinese lady gave up. She got up one final time—this time to go to the toilet. Just as she was walking slowly and struggling to the toilet, a sudden blackout hit the ward. Rooted to where she was standing, she started to grope desperately in the dark, trying to turn back to her bed, moving in frail baby steps and lamenting, "Mau berak pun susah" (I can't even go to the toilet to defecate in peace).

Everyone in the ward who was awake at that time could not help laughing at her words, the poor lady. Although I never meant to inconvenience her, I am tinged with some feelings of guilt today.

Those were among the moments of relief that I shall always cherish. It was those moments that let me know I was still alive, that the world was still revolving and that there were other people whose lives sucked too. Life was moving on in its natural pace. It renewed my strength to know that I was not alone in this.

Oni was with me all the way. She graciously and generously sacrificed her weekends to take care of me in hospital, when she could have stayed at home, comfortable and with her young children. On Sunday when we returned to our homes, I would be resting in bed and going back to school to teach, whilst she would resume her duties as wife and mother, running her home and taking care of her three young girls and tending to her husband—never-ending chores. There was simply no rest for her. But never once did she show her regret for volunteering to take care of me on top of her busy schedule at home.

There are not many persons like that here on earth. I may have been terminally ill, but I was surely blessed to have my sister Oni. And I could only pray from that day onwards and till the day I die—may God bless this special person, and may God reward her for all the love and sacrifice she has given me.

However, it would be a lie if I were to portray IPD as being all fun and adventurous. It is an experience to savour definitely—but it's certainly no joyride. To this day, I still cringe at the thought of IPD. As I have said time and again, it is something I would not wish to happen even to my enemies, if I had any.

There were times too when nothing seemed to go right with IPD. In IPD, fluid is brought into the peritoneal cavity via a PD catheter placed just underneath the layer of skin into the cavity. As with any invasive procedure, care must be taken not to allow any possibility of pathogen invasion via the cut made. One of the more unfortunate complications of IPD is when the site does get infected.

And it happened to me.

It was during one of my IPD sessions that I was unfortunate enough to get peritonitis—a condition when the peritoneum becomes inflamed as it gets infected with pathogen. The pain was simply agonising—on top of the dull pain of having already had a catheter inserted into the abdomen. The infection was bad enough to leave me prostrating in pain. I became pallid, and my abdomen became so tender that all I could do was groan in pain for the forty-eight hours I was on dialysis.

When the dialysis session was completed, I nearly blacked out in pain as the doctor pulled the catheter out of my body. I doubled over and just could not straighten my legs after that. Drawing my knees up to my chest seemed the only way to get some form of relief from the tormenting pain. For the first time since I'd started going to the hospital during the weekends, I was not anxious to be discharged immediately after the tube was pulled out of me. In fact, I was glad to be allowed to rest a little longer after I was put on antibiotics to help fight the infection.

Mercifully, the antibiotics worked, and within a few days, I was cured.

Then there was this time when, for reasons I'm not sure of, the doctor who did the IPD procedure must have punctured a blood vessel in my abdomen as well. Thus, as the dialysis fluid entered my body, blood was steadily backflowing into the tube of the catheter. The whole tube was bloody. It worried me, and I asked my sister to enquire why my tube was bloody. The nurse told me she would alert the doctor on call. Meanwhile, I was slowly but surely losing blood, up to a point where my blood pressure must have dropped so low that I could hardly sit up. Each time I tried to sit up, my head would spin, and I would come crashing back down. Things just did not feel right.

When one of the younger doctors on call came to have a look, I decided to ask her directly. "Why am I losing blood? I am beginning to feel light-headed."

"Not to worry. This is normal," was her reply, which I found very condescending and exasperating.

What?

I was really piqued by her answer. Come on! Please do not patronise me. I could accept if she had just said that sometimes these things do happen, which could not be explained. But to say that it was normal? My brain refused to accept that answer. It was not normal. That was the last straw for me. Gathering whatever strength I had left in me, I looked her straight in the eyes and said in the most serious voice I could muster, "Doctor, I am sick, but I am not stupid. Losing blood this way is not normal." Then I passed out.

I consider myself a mild individual who readily listens to anything the doctor says. I believe I am someone who is open to suggestions and advice. But if I can say this now, I feel strongly that doctors should do the best they can not to have a condescending attitude towards their patients. Be empathetic, by all means, but do not underestimate us. And don't assume that because we are ill, we therefore have lower mental faculties too.

Later that very evening, Dr Zaki made his rounds, which to me, was a godsend. The moment my sister saw him, she rushed up to him. "Dr Zaki, my sister has been leaking blood into her tube from the moment she started her IPD session. She is having blackouts, and I am getting very worried. Can you have a look at her please?"

I supposed I must have looked really emaciated and drawn back when Dr Zaki came to check on me. Immediately, he spoke to the nurse accompanying him. "Get her two pints of blood," he instructed.

And not a moment too soon, I thought, for I was beginning to feel sucked into a black depth, and I was just simply too tired to resist.

That was one of the lowest moments in my experience with IPD. I was no hero. I could feel I had no more fight left in me to put up a brave front. My body could not take much more of the IPD sessions. I just wanted to get through the whole ordeal and then sleep. If I survived at all, that would be fine; but if I didn't, I believed that it would be no great loss either. Doubt began to fill my senses. Did I really have to go through all this? Wouldn't death be a blessed relief? I had to go through all this pain and suffering week after week, and for what? I did not have many obligations in life. Life is about living in the moment—yet I was hardly living any life. The hospital was becoming my second home, where I spent every weekend hooked up to a dialysis tube. In school, I was not given much of a chance to be a real teacher. I was only given the substitute classes, understandably, considering my vulnerable and degenerating state of health. And what about my sister Oni? I was dragging her into my problem. She had enough on her hands taking care of her husband and three girls. I just did not feel like fighting anymore. I was simply a burden to everyone.

Then I looked at my sister as she sat beside me, tirelessly taking care of me, never a word of complaint. She was sacrificing her precious time to be with me at the hospital, looking after me when she could have well spent that time being home with her husband and daughters. Yet there was never any hint of giving up or regret on her face. She always looked her bubbly self, the mischievous smile on her face. She tolerated all my grumpiness and my sullen moments and gave me space when I cried in self-sympathy. She was always there, always nearby.

Oni had once told me, "There is never any doubt in my mind that you will be well one day and that you will live a normal life again."

I was there at the hospital because I was terminally ill and needed treatment. There was no need for my sister to be there. But she was—and she was committed to her task. I began to wonder. Here I was, so lucky to have a sister taking care of me, treating me like she would her own child, and all the while, I was already registered on the transplant list with a confirmed donor; it would seem that I had all the good things coming my way. Why then was I thinking of giving up? Why couldn't I just bear all this for a little bit longer?

I remember every now and then I would let out silent tears on the hospital bed, not wishing to let my sister see me broken down and disheartened. She was not giving up on me. Why then was I giving up on myself?

Those were the times I made my silent prayers to God, to beg for continued strength and patience to bear His trials and to pray that He would ease my burden so that I might carry the load I was under. I could only pray that He was pleased with my patience.

My prayers must have been heard, for they were answered. For no known reason, despite the long waiting list, my name was suddenly up for the fistula procedure. Having the fistula on my body would enable me to do the haemodialysis that would end all my sufferings with IPD.

I realised then that God is always near and He is ever watchful and ever hearing. I realised this, and it strengthened my belief that all the trials and tests that He put me through were for me to discover myself and to get closer to Him, to see Him in true light—that He gives and forgives, and that man gets and forgets. I began to realise that, in whatever trials are placed in front of us, staying on top of the game, to emerge triumphant, to a certain extent, is partly our choice. God lets us choose. And we decide whether to rise above the situation or let it destroy us. I hold on dear to the words of God in the Holy Quran:

> And no soul doth God place a burden greater than it can bear. It gets every good that it earns, and it suffers every ill that it earns. (Pray) "Our Lord! Condemn us not if we forget or fall into error, our Lord! Lay not on us a burden like that which Thou didst lay on those before us, Our Lord! Lay not on us a burden greater than we have strength to bear. Blot out our sins and grant us forgiveness. Have mercy on us. Thou art our Protector; help us against those who stand against Faith." (The Cow [Al Baqarah] 2:286)

CHAPTER

11

—

CAPD

Prayer is powerful;
but remember God works in His timing,
not yours.
Have patience.

There is a saying that, when you're at your lowest, then there's only one way left to go—up. All praise to God for answering my prayers in my moment of desperation. By His Grace, after ten episodes of intermittent peritoneal dialysis, the IPD, I was suddenly given the good news that I had been selected to enrol for the CAPD programme—continuous ambulatory peritoneal dialysis.

CAPD required that I exercise extra care of my personal hygiene and my home, particularly the room where I would perform the exchange of dialysis fluids periodically. For this purpose, whilst I was placed on an intensive training programme to learn how to perform the CAPD on my own, my husband and brother went out to order a customised 'IV stand' specifically to hook up my dialysis bag.

Patients were selected to enrol for the CAPD training programme at that time. Dr Zaki had told me that I was selected.

"There is a new brand of dialysis fluid that we are trying out for CAPD. So, I am enrolling you to learn how to perform CAPD using this brand. We will enrol you for a one-week training and teach you how to perform CAPD at home. You won't need to go through IPD again."

I was so grateful to be one of the lucky ones and looked forward to being admitted to the ward for the training—anything to take me off the IPD. I had undergone ten sessions of IPD, and the skin below my navel was running out of space for puncture marks.

Prior to the training, however, I first had to undergo a minor surgical procedure to insert the catheter, where it would stay permanently for the duration of the time I was on CAPD. The catheter had a "tap", and it would be inserted into my peritoneal cavity just like when I did my IPD. This tap would allow me to perform my dialysis fluid exchange wherever I was.

The procedure for insertion of the catheter did not take long. But just like with IPD, I still had to endure being "stabbed" for that one last time. (Later on, the area around the skin where the cut was made got infected but only superficially. Still, the infection had to be treated and cleaned, leaving a deep scar today—a lifelong reminder of my rendezvous with intermittent peritoneal dialysis.)

In the surgery room, I suppose the excitement to perform CAPD and be done with IPD once and for all drowned all my fears and anxiety. It was to be a minor surgery, involving a small vertical cut below my navel and another small insertion on my right side, also just slightly below my navel. Unfortunately, when the surgeon told me to relax as he pushed the catheter in once again, it was IPD all over again. Even the local anaesthesia could not tone down the pain at being stabbed. I comforted myself with the thought that that was to be the last stabbing I had to endure.

The CAPD provided me the chance to live as near a normal life as I could get. Throughout my CAPD days, I led an almost normal existence—except for the four times every day when I was reminded that I was, in fact, still a renal failure patient when I needed to change my dialysis fluids.

In CAPD, once the catheter was inserted permanently, I had dialysis fluid within my peritoneal cavity inside my body all the time. This ensured that my body was cleansed twenty-four hours a day—hence, the term "continuous". I had to drain off the dialysis solution sloshing in my peritoneal cavity after six hours, within which time the toxic wastes in my blood would have had enough time to be removed into the fluid to be substituted by the useful minerals my body needed. Once drained off, fresh dialysis solution needed to be filled back again into my peritoneal cavity. The exchange of dialysis fluid had to be done in the most stringent condition. My hands needed to be thoroughly cleansed to handle the taps that linked my body to the dialysis fluid bag to prevent infection. I had suffered peritonitis once before and I was anxious not to experience it again, God forbid. And so, I gave my 100 percent attention to learning the CAPD procedure. There simply was no room for slack or neglect.

For starters, I had to wash my hands for five minutes at least. The timing had to be taken seriously. It was five minutes of scrubbing my fingers and underneath my fingernails with soap and water. Once this was done, I had to apply antiseptic on both hands. Then I had to sit down in a room that had been scrubbed clean with disinfectant. First, I would have to remove the used dialysis fluid.

Once I was comfortably seated in my chair, I would take the dialysis bag from my waist pouch and hang it on the lower hook of the custom-made stand, specially tailored by my husband and my older brother Zafik. The stand had two hooks, one hook as low as possible so that, when the tap was turned on, gravity would draw as much water as possible from my peritoneal cavity into the empty dialysis bag, bringing along with it all the toxic waste accumulated over the six-hour period. This might take up to fifteen minutes. And I would just stop all activities and wait quietly until the bag was nearly full. At this point, it would usually weigh more than the original dialysis solution initially contained in the bag before it was drained into my abdomen. The excess weight would be from the fluid in my body that my kidneys could no longer remove. These moments of drawing out the used dialysis fluid were real lessons in patience and forbearance.

Next, I would detach the bag from the tap and immediately be on standby to connect a new dialysis bag filled with fresh dialysis solution. Once the tube was inserted into the new bag of dialysis fluid, I would hang it on the upper hook of the stand and turn on the tap so that, this time, the fresh dialysis fluid would enter my peritoneal cavity via the catheter. Again, I would have to wait patiently until all the fluid had entered the body, turn off the tap, fold the bag neatly, and then wrap it inside a nylon stocking and tie the stocking back around my waist. (Nowadays I believe they have come up with a special CAPD belt to keep the dialysis bag neatly secured and tucked around the waist.)

In total, the process would take about thirty minutes; and then I was free to go about my daily activities like everyone else—hence the term "ambulatory". The dialysis solution would then dwell in my abdomen for six hours, doing the job of continuously removing the toxic wastes in my body—a job my kidneys would do if they were not impaired.

Throughout this exchange procedure, I would not speak, and preferably, no one was allowed into the dialysis room. I tried to adhere to the rules as stringently as possible to avoid possible complications.

This procedure needed to be done four times each day—at 12 midnight, 6 a.m., 12 noon, and 6 p.m. Those were the times most suitable for me. I was teaching in the afternoon session then. And the afternoon supervisor of the school where I was teaching at that time, Madam Ishah, was a very understanding woman as to allow me to come in a little late and go home a little early. That was indeed a lucky break for me for, which I am grateful for to this day.

The use of CAPD gave me newfound freedom. Having the dialysis fluid within me continually day in and day out meant that the dialysis fluid would readily remove whatever toxic metabolic wastes I produced. That meant that I could go back to eating the foods I liked and eat a little bit more of them. And indeed, that became the doctor's orders too.

"Now that you're on CAPD, you can eat more and try to reach the body weight that will put you in good stead for your renal transplant operation. Try to eat more protein; maybe eat more meat to build some muscle."

After such a long while, I got the chance to eat protein foods and eat more. I finally had the luxury of eating good home-cooked steak prepared by my older sister Kak Mah, the food expert. Her cooking was always delicious and appetising. It came as no surprise when once she even won the national baking competition. Her sweet desserts, especially her moist chocolate cakes, were to die for. It was another blessing for me that, all throughout my CAPD tour, Kak Mah would make sure I always ate right.

Kak Mah is starkly different from me. She is very fair and always cheerful and friendly, just as her cooking is always delicious every time. I lived not too far from her at that time, so whenever I was not teaching, I would be at her house where her maid, Noor, and her only child, Ita, would keep me company. My niece Ita was, back then, a mischievous little girl who never failed to keep me amused with her antics.

All in all, my improved state of health made me feel more alive on the inside, and I could feel I was slowly getting back my old self.

Just to make sure I stayed in good health continuously, I still refrained from very rich foods like durian. But I would say now, in recollection, CAPD was the time during my renal failure days when I felt most lively and cheerful. Much to my delight, I even gained weight, going from thirty-three kilograms to forty kilograms. I was definitely becoming my old self once again.

CAPD also meant I was free to move about. Except for the four times when I was hooked up to the stand, I was free for the rest of the day. My husband and I arranged so that we could go out in between those "hook-up" times. If we went visiting family members and planned to stay overnight, we would bring with us the stand, which was detachable, and all the other CAPD paraphernalia. Relatives whose houses we were visiting would help us out by disinfecting one corner of their homes to allow me to do my CAPD exchange in a sterile environment when the time came. Even then, whenever I did the exchange session, no one was allowed to come near me. I would still go through the normal strict regime for safety purposes, from the word go right up to the point when the bag was finally secured around my waist.

My CAPD sessions always seemed to fascinate my young nieces and nephews though. All of them were given strict instructions not to enter the area where I did my CAPD exchange. If I was in a room, some of them would hang around at the door and watched me as I exchanged the bags, turning on and off the tap that jutted through my abdomen. I could see they were curious by the oft-repeated questions they would ask.

"What is that, Makcik Adik?" one would ask, pointing to the dialysate bag. (I am known as Makcik Adik [Little Aunt] to my nieces and nephews.)

"Oh, that is so much water. Where is all that water coming from, Makcik Adik? From inside you?"

"Are you going to bring all that water in the bag into your body now, Makcik Adik?"

I tried to answer them as briefly as I could to avoid talk as much as possible when I was doing my procedure. When they sensed my hesitation in answering their questions, they would whisper among themselves whilst pointing towards me. It almost always made me smile to watch the earnest expressions on their faces as they figured out for themselves what I was doing. And when I was finally done, with my stocking tied securely around my waist, I would rise and greet them, touching them on their soft cheeks, and they would all smile happily back at me and, may I add, almost kindly, with a touch of sympathy. I was always close to my little nieces and nephews, and even now when they are grown up and have children of their own, I feel just as attached to them as when they were little boys and girls way back then.

Life was good during my tour of CAPD. I gained weight. I was more energetic. And much to my delight, I was mobile. I did not have to be admitted to the hospital during the weekends any longer. I was more cheerful and more optimistic and was focusing on keeping myself fit and strong for my transplant, which was due in June. Most importantly, I could finally give my beloved sister Oni a break. God knew she needed it.

Fully aware and appreciative of having given the chance to do CAPD and get off the IPD, I was always vigilant to the letter. Yet, there were times that I was hard-pressed to stay awake at midnight for my fluid exchange procedure. Staying up alone when all is quiet in the middle of the night, I found that there were times when I accidentally dozed off and awakened only just in the nick of time. Once or twice, I accidentally fell asleep, only to wake up at one in the morning and had to rush through the bag exchange. Those times really educated me in self-discipline and the importance of punctuality. I would make it a practice to go to bed early and wake up just before midnight to perform the CAPD and then go back to bed again. The afternoon and the 6 p.m. sessions were not too bad, and I seldom felt harassed or rushed.

The worst part about CAPD must surely be during the early morning hours of the dialysis fluid exchange. At 6 a.m., the room was cool, and the fresh dialysis fluid in the bag was cold. The waste fluid that left my peritoneal cavity was warm, having been in my 37^0C body for six hours—only to be shocked so suddenly with an inflow of two litres of cold fresh dialysis fluid. I am sure one can hazard a guess what the sudden change of temperature would do to my bowel during the wee morning hours. The thirty minutes would be like an endless moment of sheer torture as I struggled my very best to contain myself.

Anyone who has ever been in these "real emergency" moments when you feel you really have to go and empty your bowel but cannot, will understand the mental strength I had to summon at that precise moment—the saliva building up in the mouth, the hairs on the arms standing on ends, and the face contorted in agony as I tried to contain the absolute feeling of urgency.

And when I was finally done with the exchange procedure and the bag securely tied around my waist, my husband would always ensure that nothing stood in my path to the lavatory! Hell hath no fury like a woman in urgent need of a loo.

Things were looking good for me with CAPD. My scheduled transplant date was drawing near. I had gained a few kilos in weight, and my disposition was more cheerful and positive. The numerous tests my sister had to go through to determine her state of health and the compatibility of her organ with mine were all nearly completed, and the results were favourable.

Meanwhile, my fistula for haemodialysis remained in good condition, ready to be used. Once the surgical fistula made on my left wrist had healed, I had diligently exercised it by squeezing a small ball with my left palm. The constant squeezing forces the blood to pass through the fistula and eventually makes it strong and vibrant. Anyone who touched it might easily be misled into believing that I had an electronic "buzz" implanted into my wrist. The fast-flowing blood through the fistula felt exactly like that. My husband would even get a mental "electrical jolt" every time he accidentally touched it.

Everything seemed set to go as scheduled. I just needed to clear this persistent cough I was having. I did not notice the concerned look on the doctor's face. A chest X-ray was done, and a sputum test was ordered, with three samples taken. And then we waited.

It was like a bombshell when the news was told to me.

"The sputum test results are back. I am afraid you have contracted pulmonary tuberculosis. We must treat that first before we can go through the renal transplant." Dr Zaki broke the news to me.

Oh no! Postpone my transplant? I had come so close! How could this have happened? I could not for the life of me figure out how and where I could have contracted pulmonary tuberculosis.

I felt punched in the stomach, pained, and confused. I had been rigorous in taking care of my general health. My life was only to school and back for most part of the time. I primarily mingled only with my family members. I did not shop much, as I was careful not to expose myself too much to the public, for fear of this very thing happening.

But what could I say? We plan, God decides. And His will becomes my decree.

God has said in the Holy Quran several times:

> Be, and it is. So, glory be to Him in whose Hand lies control over all things. It is to Him that you will all be brought back. (Ya Sin 36:82–3)

I recall someone mentioned to me that God must surely want me near to Him to place me in one trial after another. I remember the saying of our Holy Prophet Muhammad (peace be upon him):

> There is no pain without the expiation of sins. (Bukhari)

I was reminded of this again when I first found out about my pulmonary tuberculosis infection. God had decided I should bear His trials and tribulations a bit longer. In the Quran, we read:

> Allah will not test you with more than that you can bear. (The Cow [Al Baqarah] 2:286.)

Another Hadith of Prophet Muhammad (peace be upon him) further supports this:

If you wish to be close to Allah and His prophet,
be prepared for trials and tribulations. (Bukhari)

"How long will the transplant be postponed?" I remember asking Dr Zaki. I was not feeling the slightest bit optimistic.

"The regime for the treatment of tuberculosis is normally for either six or twelve months. We will put you on the six-month long course of chemotherapy first, and we'll see how things go," Dr Zaki told me quietly.

So that was it. My transplant was to be postponed for at least that length of time.

To make things worse, it was no longer CAPD for me. What had happened was that, as my supposed transplant date drew near, the catheter was taken out, and I was put on haemodialysis. What was supposed to be a short-term haemodialysis prior to transplant became an extended tour of dialysis on the haemodialysis machine.

Here we go again, I thought dismally.

I was never referred to the tuberculosis centre. Instead, the doctors from the nephrology department started me off on a treatment of isoniazid and rifampicin. The first experience with the chemotherapy was quite unsettling. I started to experience some bad headaches that really disrupted my daily routines. In the earlier stages, I even fainted once in school after taking the medicines in the afternoon. The school immediately called my husband, and I was taken home to rest.

This is the thing with life. It's like the turning wheels of a moving car. Life is dynamic. There are not always the up moments. Nor are there only the perpetual down moments. There are days when the sun shines brightly; there are also cloudy days.

Who should I blame when things did not go the way I wanted them to—the wheels because they are circular or the clouds for hiding the sun? And even if I could complain, what good would it bring me? Would the clouds bow down to my command? Or don't they only bow down to the will of God? Reality is that the clouds will not budge even an inch just because I complain.

So, who then did I blame? Would it bring any good if I blamed God for letting all these things happen? More importantly, what right did I have to complain at all—when He was the master, and I was a mere slave? Isn't that the essence of Islam—the complete surrender to Allah under any circumstances?

That very same God Who had created me in the first place had breathed life into me so that I could live and feel love and learn humility and kindness. Was it right that I should suddenly turn around and condemn Him after all the blessings He had bestowed upon me? When He is my Creator, what right did I have to protest? As easily as He created me, I knew without a doubt, He could easily demolish me as He pleased.

We are totally at His Mercy. If we learn to accept this, that will surely spare us any grief and dissatisfaction. That One God does not leave us alone in our struggles in this life. In Islam, we believe He has left us guidance in the form of the Holy Quran—our manual to live by successfully in this life and to overcome kinks in our lives and how to be successful in the hereafter. He has taught us to continually to remember Him in times of calamity:

> Those who have faith and whose hearts find
> peace in the remembrance of God—truly it is in
> the remembrance of God that hearts find peace.
> (Thunder [Ar Ra'd] 13:28)

Furthermore, if we just take some time to ponder this a little bit further, we see that God has created us at His will, but He does not create us in vain and leave us to be in a state of total helplessness. He has given us ample provision—the air we breathe, the sun and the wind, food sources, and water. He has given us faculties that allow us to be sensitive to our surroundings and to adjust ourselves accordingly. He has instilled in us love in its various forms—that of a man or a woman, a son or a daughter, a father or a mother, a brother or sister, a servant of God. Above all else, He has given us intelligence—the faculties of thought and reflection—to identify how servants should behave towards their Lord and master. Even then, by His mercy, He has given us enough freedom to choose—to be grateful servants and succumb to His will in full submission, confident of His succour or to deny and defy His supremacy.

Was I dejected to have my transplant postponed for another six months? Of course, I was. I was devastated. I had looked forward to it and prayed hard for it. That was my ticket to a new lease on life—there was no telling if I would survive the next six months. But what good would it do if I were to whine and complain? I was just a mere servant of God; it was His will that I did not get my transplant done just yet. But it was also His will that I was still alive. I just needed to have full faith that He knew best. This was just another test from Him, another hurdle that I knew would bring me closer to Him. I just had to truly put my trust in Him—that all these things happening to me were indeed blessings in disguise, for the betterment of my soul, if nothing else.

It was these thoughts that comforted me and gave me the strength to accept my fate. My transplant was postponed; that was the will of God. But I was still alive and still able to enjoy life's little pleasures. There was always hope yet, for as long as I put my faith in God and His Mercy and love. The helpless feeling inside me left me no alternatives but to turn to Him, for only He could understand my devastation. He made me get close to Him and seek His mercy and help. At that point, in my moment of utter despair and frustration, was when I felt closest to Him, praying constantly and even harder to Him. It was His will that I was drawn closer to Him by the trials He had placed on me. I knew He was watching over me, and even though it may seem He was just making my life difficult, I could feel that I was actually being taught the meaning of total submission and acceptance to His will and that, as long as I believed in His will, there would always be hope.

For all the small miracles in life that He had placed before me and despite my illness, I say these words:

Then which of the favours of your Lord will ye deny? (The Lord of Mercy [Ar Rahman] 55:13)

This experience of feeling totally helpless and of putting all the trust I had in God isn't easy to explain in words. Despite my frustration, the feeling left me with a strangely quiet and comforting calmness. It was a moment when I felt very close to God—a sense of total submission. It gave me the strength to be grateful, despite the predicament I was in.

For all the good things in life, I am grateful, so bless me God, for all the trials and tribulations that you have laid before me. I seek forgiveness and pray for your Mercy upon me.

What I was going through might seem a series of bad luck—one setback after another. But what people could not see was what I felt in the heart—the mercy of God, whose presence was so near when I was ill, so closely felt in my desperate hours of need.

12

Off to Haemodialysis

Everything is going to be all right;
maybe not today, but eventually.

And so it was. Instead of going to the operating table for a renal transplant, I was sent to the haemodialysis unit in Kuala Lumpur Hospital (HDU HKL). And once again, my life was tied to the hospital—this time literally to a quietly buzzing machine that would busily cleanse my blood as I sat hooked to it.

My six-month therapy for my tuberculosis denied me the appointed date for renal transplant. The CAPD catheter had already been removed, and the hospital had no intention of reinserting another one. I was sent to the haemodialysis unit (HDU) to start my tour of haemodialysis, which would take at least six months, or for as long as I needed treatment for my pulmonary tuberculosis.

The HDU building was, at that time, located right at the end of the nephrology clinic and wards, near the car park, quite isolated. The first time I went there, I was suspicious of the quietness of the place; there did not seem to be any activities around. However, when I entered the actual dialysis room, I was surprised to find rows of haemodialysis machines on either side of the room, humming away busily and occasionally even letting out a high-pitch beep, giving one the feel of hustle and bustle and just the ordinary rush of activities. Nurses and hospital aids walked briskly about their business. Some patients would be busy and skilfully getting themselves ready to be hooked up to the machine, whilst others, already settled in, reclined back in their chairs and watched all the activities pass by them.

I went up to the counter, where a slimly built Malay nurse with fair skin and light brown eyes was working and handed her my appointment letter. As she read through my letter, I noticed from her name tag that her name was Asmah. When she had finished reading, she then called out to a male nurse (or HA perhaps they were called). There were no smiles or small talk. Asmah was as brisk and serious as she looked.

"Ahmad, we have a new patient here. Can you prepare the last machine for this lady, please?"

Ahmad smiled quietly at me and immediately walked to the back of the room to prepare my machine. Meanwhile I was ushered to one corner of the room to have myself weighed and my blood pressure taken and then recorded into my newly opened haemodialysis file.

Ahmad led me to the farthest end of the room—to the only available machine left. Wide-eyed, I watched in fascination as he deftly attached tubes to the machine, which was humming quietly. It felt as if the machine was greeting me and sizing me up as well. A strange cylindrical tube with one end red and the other end blue was then attached to the machine as well.

My curiosity got the better of me and I started asking questions. "What is that cylinder for?"

"This is the 'false kidney'. It takes over the task of your kidneys to filter and remove toxic wastes from you blood," Ahmad explained.

Hmm … a man-made kidney to replace the ones God had given me and then taken back (due to my neglect, I am sure), I mused ruefully. I tried seeking some solace from the blue-red cylinder that was to be my lifesaver.

I remember watching in amazement as Ahmad went about his work—fixing connecting lines and tubes to the machine and then flushing the tubes with fluid after pushing different buttons on the machine. My illness was temporarily forgotten.

So, this was to be my lifeline until my next opportunity to be back on the renal transplant list. I was to depend on this machine for the next six months at least, coming to this HDU three times a week to cleanse my blood and body of toxic wastes in my effort to remain alive.

Since I was teaching in the afternoon session, I was put on the Tuesday-Thursday-Saturday morning shifts. That was the arrangement that would disturb my teaching routine the least. On these days, I would leave home as early 6.15 a.m. to undergo dialysis for four hours and, hopefully, be fit enough afterwards to get to school.

My fascination was gently interrupted as Ahmad told me to sit on the black reclining chair. The chair was comfortable, with a footrest so I could lift my feet up. I was about to be hooked onto the machine for the next four hours. Feeling nervous and a little anxious to embark into a hitherto unknown territory, I braced myself as Ahmad pulled up my sleeve to insert not one but two needles into my left arm where my AV fistula was.

As he pushed in the needles one after another, Ahmad briefly explained what was about to happen. "One of the needles here will be attached to the tube that will carry the blood out of your body to the machine for dialysis. This other one is for the return of the cleansed blood back into your body."

And this was where the fistula played its part. The fistula was created for dialysis access. It is an enlarged vein created by connecting an artery directly to a vein. Connecting the artery to the vein allowed a much greater blood flow into the vein. As a result, the vein enlarged and strengthened, making inserting of needles for haemodialysis treatment easier.

Once all the tubes were attached in the right places and I was securely hooked to the dialysis machine, Ahmad told me to relax and lie back while he slowly opened the valve from the line. I watched, entranced, as my blood slowly started to leave my arm, running along the tube towards the haemodialysis machine. I could feel the gush of blood as it left my body into the machine until it reached the false kidney cylinder where it would be cleansed.

It was a strange sensation to watch my blood leave my body and go into the tubes and then to the cylinder—a wistful feeling accompanies knowing that your body has permanently lost a part of its functions and that you have become dependent on a machine to continue with your existence. As I leaned back against the sofa and resigned myself to the upcoming four hours of dialysis, I began to contemplate.

How had I gotten into this predicament?

Where would I be if I were not put on this dialysis programme—if I were not hooked to this blinking beeping machine?

What were the odds that I would make it through this time?

At the same time, there was this feeling of awe that I was living in an era where science has advanced so much that it had helped mankind cheat death just that bit longer. I tell myself again and again that I am a living testimony to the wonders of science, by God's grace of course, for it is "He who gives and takes away life." Until I retired, at every opportunity when I was teaching, I tried to instil this awareness in all my students. Until the day I retired, teaching this particular topic to my biology students made me feel ever so enthusiastic and nostalgic at the same time.

For this very first tour of haemodialysis, I had come in the afternoon and clocked in at nearly three. That meant my first ever session of dialysis would end by seven in the evening. I tried to settle down as comfortably as I could and started looking around at the other patients. Most of them were asleep or at least had their eyes closed, apparently lulled by the quiet humming of the machines in the room. I was the new kid on the block—so many things to gawk at. Once or twice, I could feel the machine tugging at the tubes running across my arm, and I noticed that my movements had caused kinks in the lines. I carefully straightened my arm so as not to block the blood flow to and from the machine. I was certainly not prepared to face any mishaps on my very first day of haemodialysis.

Prior to coming for my haemodialysis, I had eaten a rather hearty meal, knowing that I was about to undergo dialysis anyway. Initially I did not feel much difference, but when I entered the last hour of dialysis, my stomach began to churn rather uncomfortably. And then came the headache! The sharp pain felt as if someone was pressing on both sides of my temples with all his might. I very well nearly threw up from the nausea and pain I was experiencing. I just wanted to cradle my head, trying to ease the pain. But no matter how I turned my head, the pain simply refused to abate. My head felt like I was drying up on my inside, ready to blow up at any moment. I looked at my watch that I had taken off and placed on the small table beside me; it was the longest half hour of my life waiting for my four-hour session to end. My head felt close to exploding. The pain was just too strong.

By the time it was over and one of the nurses came to unhook me, my body felt like a worn-out rag doll. I simply could not stand up without faltering. My head was spinning rapidly; I was feeling uncomfortably warm in the air-conditioned room and nauseous. I remember staggering to the front desk to have my blood pressure and weight reading taken once again. I just wanted to rest my head on someone's shoulder and cry my heart out in self-pity. It was all I could do to prevent myself from bursting into tears when my husband walked in to take me home. I did cry, though, once we were in the car. I remember telling him through my tears, "I don't know how I am going to get through this every other day," all the time cradling my tender head.

As clear as daylight, I can still remember the persistent headache that would not leave and the uncomfortably warm feeling throughout my body. It felt like being trapped in a hot sauna but not being able to break into a sweat. Yet somehow, I managed to hold back my stomach content until I got home. Once I got to the toilet, the waves of convulsion came one after the other, leaving me completely exhausted afterwards. Thankfully, it did help ease the terrible headache a little.

I slept all the way through that night, oblivious to everything around me—the sleep of true exhaustion. But it was not before I allowed, once again, the tears to take over me, wondering when all this would stop and if there were still worse things to come. I prayed for strength and patience, although I wasn't feeling too confident at the moment.

After one week of aided haemodialysis, Ahmad gave me a surprise.

"Norhafizah, today you are going to learn how to prepare the machine yourself. We don't know when you will get your renal transplant, so it will be good for you to be in control of your machine," Ahmad explained.

I could only nod, starting to feel a bit anxious about doing all this on my own.

Ahmad started with the false kidney.

"You will be using one false kidney three times before you change to a new one. So later we will teach you how to clean your tubes and kidney and where to store them."

That really got me worried. All the haemodialysis sessions I'd gone through in the past week had left me terribly exhausted and incapacitated by the terrible headaches afterwards. I was practically staggering just to stand up and get off the chair every time. Now I was expected to clean up the tubes and false kidney after each dialysis session? Could I possibly cope?

Yet, whilst it worried me a bit to be doing things on my own, I must admit I got very excited about the challenge of preparing my own machine. The most exciting part to me was that I even had to learn to insert the two needles myself. It was a challenge I could not resist and could not wait to master. It meant that I could adjust the insertion so they would not hurt me. It also meant gaining some independence from the hospital assistants and taking charge of my own treatment once again.

Whenever I was introduced to something new that arouses my curiosity, I would be a very eager and fast learner. That's just how I am. So, I must thank God that it was not too difficult for me to grasp what HA Ahmad taught me that morning, especially when he explained the rationale for each step of the procedure. Finally, we came to the point when I was, for the first time, about to insert the two needles into my left arm. Ahmad was being considerate. I had a lot to soak in already.

"You know, if you think you have had too much to learn today, we can try doing the needles next time," he suggested kindly.

"Oh no! I want to try it now please," I rushed to answer.

Truth be told, that was really the highlight of the whole learning process for me—to be truly independent and self-resilient. At that time, after my fling with IPD, I never considered myself as being weak-hearted when in face of a challenge, and I wanted to prove that to myself. I told Ahmad I was ready.

Steadily and gently, Ahmad led me to feel my own veins and told me that I would not feel much pain if I managed to get the needle right into the lumen of the vein and not get it stuck in the wall. Then he said something very profound that I have not forgotten until today.

"The good thing about puncturing your arm by yourself is that you know when you are ready and not to give pain to yourself. You take your time; just insert the needle when you are well and ready."

Ahmad was absolutely right. Since that moment, I did my own insertion of needles, and they were painless every time. The numerous needle marks on my left arm today bear witness to the times I inserted those needles inside me for my haemodialysis and my left arm today looking like that of a drug addict's. It is difficult to describe the sense of independence I felt. It was certainly liberating. I was basically in control of my own self.

The other good thing that came from handling the machine and the whole procedure by myself was that I got to manipulate the heparin volume. Heparin is injected into the tube every time during haemodialysis to prevent blood clots from forming in the tube. The danger with blood clots forming in the tubes is that the clot might get dislodged within the tube and end up in my blood vessels. If by sheer bad luck it were to get stuck in any of my smaller blood vessels, I would probably end up with an embolism, God forbid.

Unfortunately, I'd learnt earlier from my haemodialysis procedure that my body was sensitive to heparin. The normal amount injected into the tube would usually find me having problems trying to stop the bleeding from my needle insertion points later on. Sometimes, on worse days, even my gums would bleed profusely. That was exhausting and frustrating. At one time, I was filled with self-pity, wondering why such goof-ups always had to happen to me. Still, the incident alerted me that controlling the heparin volume was important. I needed just enough to avoid blood clots in the tube yet prevent excessive bleeding post dialysis; it was always a precarious decision for me to make.

From then on began my tour of dialysis every alternate day except Sundays and Mondays. From the first week it was the same every time; the final hour would be the most challenging. The pressing headache would come. I would feel nauseous. And the general feeling of discomfort would soon escalate into actual physical pain.

Since I had my dialysis session in the morning, I would finish by 11.30 a.m., when I would struggle to the waiting room just outside the HDU along with some other patients. Now these patients were veterans in haemodialysis; some of them had been coming for dialysis for years and years. They would look at me sympathetically, make sure I had a seat whilst waiting for my husband, and generally treat me like their little sister. They seemed to understand the poor state I was in after dialysis and would only ask me one or two questions. Most of the time, I would just sit quietly, preferring to listen to them talk. They would be talking and laughing away as if the dialysis was just another routine task of the day. They looked so normal, not fatigued, just like some housewives on their way back from shopping at the market. Only their pale lips and dry skins gave away their reality.

Eventually I got to know most of them by name, and slowly their tragic sad stories would surface. Over time, I learnt that, for some of them, their husbands could not be patient with their present health condition and left. One patient who happened to be a nurse was left to fend for her five children after her husband left her when she was in that condition.

"His excuse was, because of my condition, I could not provide him with children," she explained cynically.

What irony! They already had five.

Another lady had her mother-in-law constantly degrading her for her illness and badgering her son to leave his sick wife.

"We have to pass this graveyard on our way home from hospital. My mother-in-law will tell my only daughter that that is where I will be buried soon," she said once with a wry smile on her face.

Apparently, she was never her mother-in-law's choice for a daughter-in-law. But surely that didn't give the mother-in-law any right to say such condemning things about my terminally ill friend. My jaw dropped. Good Lord! How could anyone be so cruel, so heartless?

I could see that, while they all appeared cheerful on the outside, in reality, they all harboured more trying moments than I did. At the same time, I saw too that they sought comfort and strength from each other, and I truly respected their solidarity.

Over time, I was absorbed into their circle, and they all became my close friends—comrades in arms so to speak. Unlike me, these were ladies who were not on the transplant list, unable to come up with donors. They may be permanently dependent on the dialysis machines for life, emotionally scarred but their spirits never broken. They were strong at heart, living through their hardships alone and without complaints. They accepted their fates and continued to fight on with their lives. There was a lot I learnt from them—most importantly, acceptance. I was certainly lucky. I had the staunch support from my parents and siblings, and my husband was very patient with the condition I was in.

Ultimately, the biggest boon in handling my own dialysis was to be able to monitor just how much water to extract throughout the four-hour procedure. I had learnt that the terrible headaches I felt during dialysis were due to the fluid being extracted by the machine. For the alternate days that I came for my dialysis, it was a rare occasion that my body weight would increase drastically. During non-dialysis days, I generally did not eat or drink much, so my weight gain was not that apparent or anything to worry much about.

The same cannot be said with some of my fellow patients. I suppose they had good appetite and so would eat normally like other normal people. Some did not bother much about controlling their diet and fluid consumption, given that they would be on dialysis every alternate day. This would inevitably result in a drastic increase in weight when they became waterlogged. This, in turn, meant they required an extraction of up to five to six kilograms at any one session of dialysis. My weight fluctuations were minimal, and so for every session, to lose two kilograms was good enough. I found out that, by controlling the extraction force, I could prevent those terrible headaches. With those terrible headaches greatly reduced, I found out my blood pressure too became more manageable.

And that is why I keep repeating to my children, my students and myself—it is always good to be knowledgeable on things that concern us.

Haemodialysis is no stroll in the park. As for myself, for four hours of my life, on alternate days, I was hooked to a machine, in a room at the far end of the hospital where the car park is. The ambience in the room was one of quiet calm, with the occasional beep from the machines to remind the patients of their dependency on those machines. The reality remained that I was there because I would simply die without the machine. The fact that my arm was hooked to the machine via those long tubes was a grim reminder that I was dependent on the machine for some functions my body had failed to carry out. And that was a sobering thought.

All that befalls us is not without reason. It is up to us to make sense of things. It is up to us to derive the good from the bad that happens in our lives. Admittedly, some would have said that the best thing would be to surrender one's fate to the hands of God—be and it shall be. I don't argue with that. Inevitably, what finally befalls us is what He has ordained and decreed in the first place. My concern was, what was my role in all this? Should I just succumb? Should I retaliate and deny? Or should I put in my best effort forward and then place my full trust in Him? God is ever ready to give us what we pray and ask Him for. The question is, are we ready to receive it?

I am not a religious person—not by a far cry. But what I do know is this—my being in that predicament at that time had a purpose, and if all it meant was for me to fight for my life, then it would be something I would do. I just had to put some effort in before I totally left my fate to God—so that I was able to tell myself, "I have done my best. Now let God do the rest."

I am reminded of this Hadith of the Holy Prophet Muhammad (peace be upon him). He reminded us to be mindful of God and always to have faith in Him. Yet on top of that, Prophet Muhammad (peace be upon him) reminded us, too, "to tie the camel first before leaving its fate into the hands of God" (At Tirmidhi).

I guess this was what Stephen Covey meant when he introduced the 90/10 principles. It's that 10 percent of what happens to us is beyond our control. The remaining 90 percent, however, is up to us; we can give up, or we can fight and do our best.

> God suffices me: There is no God save Him.
> In Him have I put my trust, and He is Lord
> of the Tremendous Throne. (Repentance [At
> Tauba] 9:129]

CHAPTER

13

———

Those Good Men and Women

==================================

One day, you'll be just a memory for some people.
Do your best to be a good one.

==================================

Alas! The temporary setback from my renal transplant
extended from six months to a year. Although I was declared
clear from pulmonary tuberculosis within the six-month therapy
regime, the doctors just wanted to be sure and were reluctant to
take any chances. (I am now on lifelong prophylaxis medication
for tuberculosis.)

And so it was, on every alternate day, for three days in a
week, my husband would drive me from our home in Petaling
Jaya to the HDU in Kuala Lumpur, a forty-five-minute drive,

before he shot off to work. To ensure I started my dialysis on time so I could finish by twelve in the afternoon, we started off very early in the day, which meant we had to leave home immediately after the Subh (dawn) prayer. That way, we would beat the morning rush hour traffic, and my husband could get to his office on time. There are, indeed, many memories I hold dear during those haemodialysis days. There were just the two of us, my husband and I, and those early morning drives I believe, brought us closer together. At this juncture, I must add that my husband was very compliant, without a word of complaint. I thank God for that.

A few previous experiences had showed me that I really could not eat much during dialysis. Eating heavily during haemodialysis would only hasten the onset of those killer headaches. It was a pity really, for whilst the machine was doing the work of my failed kidneys in removing any toxic wastes from my metabolism, that would be the best time for me to devour whatever food I may crave in any acceptable amounts. Whatever would be potentially hazardous to my condition would be dialysed out immediately. Sadly, I was not meant to enjoy that fringe benefit.

And so, that was another reason I would leave early for my haemodialysis. We would stop by at any restaurant along the route or, if we were extra early, at the hospital cafeteria for me to have my breakfast first. Again, it would not be so hearty, because a full stomach does not go well with the four-hour dialysis either, at least for me. It had to be just the right amount to put me in good stead during dialysis when my blood entered and left my body continually through the tubes attached to the machine.

After a few trials and errors, breakfast would usually be *roti telur* or *masala dosai* or a plate of fried rice, every time with a mug of hot tea. *Masala dosai* is an Indian pancake dish made from rice batter and black lentils with masala potato filling.

Then after that, I would pack some local pastries like curry puff or some soft pudding for light snacks to be nibbled throughout the duration of my dialysis.

Maybe I was too thin. Maybe I wasn't strong enough. Or maybe my body was just too sensitive. I don't know. But any off beats from this strict regime, and I would end up with the terrible headaches. In time, I learnt it would be all right for me to make small talk, but excitement or serious conversation would certainly aggravate those explosive headaches.

There was one time when I was slowly dozing off to the monotonous continuous hum of my machine, when one of the hospital assistants (HA) approached me. "I hear you are a secondary school teacher. What subject do you teach?" he asked, making light talk with me, or so I thought.

"I am supposed to teach science. But right now, I am just a relief teacher," I tried to explain as briefly as possible.

"Actually, I was wondering if you can help me with some lower secondary mathematics problem. It's for my nephew," he asked politely.

I was eager to help, happy to oblige. "Sure, let's see if I can help. Show me the problem."

The problem turned out to be simple enough to solve without much effort. It was satisfying to be able to solve the problem for him. Within a few minutes, I returned the piece of paper with the solution to him. The HA smiled with apparent relief on his face. I smiled back, but just as I started to recline back into my chair, he spoke again.

"This is great. But do you think you can explain the steps you took to solve the problem? It will make it easier for me to make my nephew understand later."

Now, being a teacher, I automatically proceeded to explain to him as I would to a fourteen-year-old, which helped the HA to grasp the steps easily enough. I could sense that he was highly appreciative from his profuse thanks.

Not so for me, unfortunately. The brief but methodical explaining and teaching left me with such a pounding headache later that I was close to cursing and shouting my head off to the poor HA, who was smiling gratefully at me each time he passed by my way. The poor chap must have been wondering why I was giving him the murderous look.

Then there was this time when I was seated next to a young Malay girl with a bubbly nature and a great sense of humour. She was the youngest and only girl of an orphaned family of all boys, and her brothers doted on her and pampered her silly. Like me, she was also on the transplant list. To have a supporting family is always a bonus to any terminal and long-term patients. It just gives you that extra boost to hang on and stay above your illness. I know I was one of those lucky ones to have the unflinching support of my sister Oni especially and my other siblings in general. And this young woman was another.

Rakiah, as the young girl was called, was always the cheerful and positive minded one, who sometimes tended to run on the mischievous side. Every time I chanced to sit beside her, it would mean four hours of listening to her incessant chatter and jokes. I was just happy to listen to her, wondering if the dialysis was affecting her at all. As for me, I have always been more comfortable being the listener than a talker.

It was one of those times when she was on dialysis seated next to me at the far end of the dialysis room, when she told me that she was going to have a feast on that day.

"What do you mean?" I remember asking her curiously.

Slowly, with a sparkle of mischief in her eyes that could not be missed and a face beaming like a child about to divulge her prized possession, she quietly opened the lid to the plastic food container on the coffee table we shared between us. "This," she finished off with a mischievous chuckle.

Immediately the rich, strong scent of durian stung my nostrils. To some, the very strong odour of this Malaysian king of fruits can be quite upsetting, enough to make them repel the fruit totally. But not so for me. I just love durians; its strong sweet aroma would surely entice me each time it whiffs through me. I would and actually literally nearly did die for one previously, unfortunately, which ultimately led me to this life of dialysis.

Before I could start speaking, suddenly from the opposite end of the room, HA Ahmad's voiced boomed. "Who has brought durians to this room? Durians are prohibited in this room—what more during dialysis!"

Rakiah hurriedly closed back the container, and we quickly pretended not to know anything of it. Ahmad walked the length of the room towards us and stopped right in front of us.

Now the strength of the scent of durian is such that the powerful odour lingers thickly in the air, even when they're not in sight. So, obviously the scent was strongest in our area. Ahmad looked at the both of us sharply, expecting one of us to own up. I guess he knew better, because he had his body turned towards Rakiah longer than towards me. I guess he knew I was always the more obedient and obliging patient.

Rakiah stared back at him, fluttering her eyelids and feigning innocence. Although my heart was beating erratically for being an accomplice, I could not help but marvel at the young girl's antics and had to desperately suppress my sniggers. Ahmad continued staring for a moment longer before he slowly turned around. As he left us, he spoke slowly, but just enough for the both of us to hear.

"No matter ... The guilty party will be found out soon enough."

I wondered what exactly he meant by those last words, but quickly brushed it aside when Rakiah opened the lid again and pushed the container towards me.

Yummyyy! The soft, smooth, rich, succulent, and thick texture of the golden flesh of the durian was, to me, like heaven on earth. I relished every single moment, savouring every single mouth-watering bite. Rakiah and I feasted to our heart's content quietly in our corner at the far end of the haemodialysis unit.

I think I was on about the third or fourth piece when suddenly I started feeling woozy and queer. My stomach felt like a churning cement grinder. My tongue tasted strange; I could not really feel it. I turned to look at Rakiah. She was not looking too good either. Her face was ashen.

And then it happened. Just as I finally grasped what HA Ahmad meant by his last statement, suddenly there was this massive force from my stomach; and just like a volcanic eruption, I began to spew out all the durians I had eaten earlier. They came in wave after wave of convulsions that seemed to go on forever. My vomit bag was full in no time. I barely noticed that Rakiah was in the same sorry state that I was.

When the retching finally stopped, I was greatly relieved to rest my tired used-up body. Rakiah too was lying back, and she looked absolutely exhausted, her eyes tightly shut. I looked past her and was greeted by the staring eyes of the other dialysis patients. And then I saw HA Ahmad approaching us in steady strides. Watching his serious face, my heart froze.

"So, now we finally know who brought the durians into this room," he said quietly, emphasising the word "who".

We were exposed for sure, but I was just too worn out to argue my case. There was, in fact, no case to argue anyway. We were guilty as charged.

Then HA Ahmad continued. "I have a good mind to increase the rate of fluid extraction from the both of you. That would make your day complete," he said cynically.

I looked up in horror. Oh no! Extracting more fluid from my already drained body would surely make the dreaded headache even worse.

Thank God he didn't. He just walked back to the front, and that was the end of it. And for that, I am grateful to HA Ahmad for always.

Indeed, there were many instances when I was grateful to the wonderful men and women working in the HDU. Initially, my first impression of them was that they had very serious looks about them—not quick to smile. In due time, I came to realise that they were mostly brisk and had the no-nonsense air about them because of the very nature of their duties. They were dealing with terminally ill patients hooked to machines for sustenance of life. At any point in time, either the patient or the machine might go faulty. And usually, these men and women working here would immediately respond to the buzzing machine and check on the patients.

Staff nurse Asmah was in charge of the patients who were on the transplant list such as myself, as well as those on the permanent dialysis list. It follows that she had to be meticulous with her work. She knew all her patients by name, what our current state of health was, and what procedures or medication the doctors had prescribed for us.

Over time, I got to learn that these men and women, despite their serious outlook, were very empathetic towards us. Whenever they noticed any one of us feeling or looking too lethargic to clean up after ourselves, they would take over, helping the patient finish off and clean and put away the false kidney. Whenever they had the luxury of a few minutes of free time, they would come over to make small talk with us.

There was this one time when I had to change my dialysis schedule to take my driving licence test. Permission was granted; I came back for my Thursday haemodialysis feeling sorry for myself for failing the test. I remember it was staff nurse Asmah who asked me about the driving test.

"I failed. During parking, I didn't hit the back pole, I hit the front pole—how pathetic!" I exclaimed, feeling quite annoyed with myself.

"When was your last dialysis?" someone asked.

That was the trouble. The driving test was on Tuesday, and the Sunday and Monday before that were non-dialysis days. It was three days without dialysis. I could only imagine the toxin level in my brain at that time. That could very possibly have clouded my senses and focus.

It was then that staff nurse Asmah, who was listening in on us, opened up. "Don't feel too bad. I took my driving test six times and failed every time," she said with a straight face. "I am not taking another one; it's just too difficult," she finished off.

Six times? Come on...

A few other patients who were also listening in found it rather hilarious, and we had a good laugh over her confession. For such a capable and efficient staff nurse, she had shown us her human side; she was not faultless after all, and somehow that earned her a new respect from all of us.

On a later date, I took the driving test again. All praise to God, I passed on my second try.

Then there was one occasion when I had too much heparin for my own good. Before every haemodialysis session, dialysis patients must inject heparin into the dialysis tube to prevent blot clots from forming in our tubes. Blood clots in the tube could pose a big danger should they get dislodged from the tube and find their way back into our bloodstream.

My body somehow could not tolerate the normal volume of heparin the others were given. What happened after dialysis was, not only did the puncture points where I inserted the needles refuse to stop bleeding when the needles were removed, but my gums had also started to bleed profusely and just would not stop. I waited for nearly three hours, and still the gums would not stop bleeding. Even the afternoon shift dialysis patients were ending their treatment.

One of the HAs took pity on me for being in the clinic for so long without food or drink (I was bleeding from the gums, and I wasn't too keen on the idea of swallowing my own blood). So I was sent to the dental department to see if they could help out.

The dentist immediately checked me out and found no cavities anywhere. The bleeding from the gums was solely due to the heparin. Ultimately, all he could do was to plaster my gums with temporary cement in an effort to stop the bleeding. Still, I was told not to consume anything till sometime later. Then and only then did the bleeding finally stop.

Since that incident, I was allowed to reduce the volume of heparin to half that of the other patients.

Now, with a smaller volume of heparin used, that posed another problem for me yet again—the tendency for the blood to clot in the tube or false kidney. It happened on one occasion; I had just started my haemodialysis when suddenly I faced some difficulty in breathing, which grew progressively worse. My heart felt like it was going into arrest. The pain was so acute I could barely cry out to get attention. God be praised, HA Ahmad was quick to notice my feeble attempts to get attention, and he was immediately by my side.

"What is the matter, Fizah?" he asked. There was an urgency in his voice.

"My chest. It feels tight. I cannot breathe," was my laborious response.

Immediately, Ahmad rushed to the reception table and came back with a capsule. "Here, put this under your tongue. I am going to stop your dialysis now."

I am just so thankful to this very day and believe his quick action helped save my life. I was experiencing something akin to heart attack, and if not for his quick action of stopping the dialysis machine and administering the medication under my tongue (glyceryl trinitrate)—if no one was around to help—I truly don't know what might have happened to me then. A doctor was called to check in on me, and I was immediately sent to the ward for further observation.

I was told that what had probably happened was that a tiny clot from the false kidney had dislodged and gotten into my blood stream, causing the temporary strain on my heart and my difficulty in breathing. Later, the dialysis staff told me it could happen to anyone, and it was not my fault. I had chastised myself severely for possibly being negligent in cleaning out my false kidney previously. It was a grim reminder for me, and I vouched to be more vigilant in future if there was to be any chance at all for me to get a renal transplant and live the life I had always dreamed of.

These quiet hard-working men and women, behind the scene, rarely get the attention of anyone. Yet they perform their duties diligently and without much complaint. I could feel at that time that our welfare was their uppermost concern. They were strict for our own good. But at times, they would let their guard down, and I would catch glimpses of their true caring nature. For that, I am ever so thankful, and I pray that, wherever they may be today, their lives be blessed always. After I got to know them, I believe they were significant in helping me get through my ordeal. Their kind and considerate nature and their compassion spared me the grief of mistreatment and assured me that my welfare was taken care of and that I was in good hands. Most importantly, I was a person in their eyes, not just another statistical data. They never gave up on any of us.

To me, this is kindness. And I am reminded of this saying by Mark Twain: "Kindness is the language which the deaf can hear and the blind can see."

CHAPTER

14

Good for Go

---

*The hardest test in life is the patience
to wait for the right moment.*

Throughout the postponement of my transplant, tests continued to be carried out to ensure I was progressively ready for the eventual moment. There were numerous blood tests, urine tests, stool analysis, and even an endoscopy. I was sent to have my oral hygiene checked and cavities filled—all in preparation for the upcoming transplant.

My sister too was subjected to stringent tests to ensure that she was in steady state of health to donate her kidney— she had repeated blood tests, a twenty-four-hour urine tests, and compatibility tests. At one point she was even selected to become a sample for a protein study. She had to go to the hospital and be subjected to a big hearty meal of protein and later analysed. Unfortunately, my sister was not a person with large appetite, and she had a hard time trying to gobble down half a roasted chicken.

Then there was the one time when she had to be admitted for an angiogram to review the condition of her kidney. She was admitted to the same nephrology ward I'd been in when I was doing my peritoneal dialysis—Ward 4A. When I visited her in the evening, she had just completed the procedure and was asked to lie immobile for at least a few hours. It felt strange to visit her; she was the patient and I, the visitor—a role reversed. But selfishly, I must admit that it felt awfully good to be the one who got to go home that night for once.

All results that came back were in favour of her being my donor, and we were set to go. It all depended on my final check on the progress of my pulmonary tuberculosis condition. Even that turned out positively encouraging. We were both ready for a renal transplant. It was just a matter of fitting into the hospital surgery schedule.

The big breakthrough came in early July when staff nurse Asmah told me I was scheduled for transplant on 26 July 1988—a Tuesday. Tuesdays were renal transplant operation days. I was eager and excited; my sister was calm and collected. Little did we know we were both in for yet another surprise.

My sister and I were patiently prepping ourselves for the day in eager anticipation.

It was on 12 July 1988 when I received the shocking news. I had just finished with my haemodialysis and cleaned my tubes when Asmah approached me.

"Fizah, I have something very important to tell you. Your name is up for transplant next week," she said with a smile.

I was stunned, speechless. I had difficulty digesting what I'd just heard. I'd been waiting all this while and now that it was just around the corner, I was speechless. When I finally got my tongue back, I remember asking simply, "How come? I thought I was scheduled for the twenty sixth."

"Well, the Indian chap who was scheduled for that date has declined to undergo surgery on that day," Asmah explained.

"But why?" I was genuinely puzzled.

"He consulted an astrologer, who prophesied that the nineteenth of July is not a good day for renal transplant. He said it would be bad luck," she continued before finishing off. "He is adamant that he will not undergo the transplant on that day. So it looks like you are next, Fizah."

All praise be to God, I am a Muslim and I do not believe in any dates as being unlucky or otherwise. What will happen will happen as the will of God. Plus, there was the fact that I was eager to have my transplant be over and done with. I accepted this change of date without any second thoughts. His bad luck could just be opportunity knocking on my door. I had been certified as fit for transplant for a few months now. My tuberculosis was clear. All the necessary tests and procedures on both my sister's and my part had been completed. We were set to go.

(As it turned out, the poor chap later had an infection, and to this day, I do not know if he went through the renal transplant at all).

Like me, Oni was stunned to learn that our transplant date had been brought forward. And like me, she too was not going to miss out on the opportunity. The sudden change of dates meant that things had to be done in a hurry though. This sudden change of plans probably took my brother-in-law by surprise. And in his shock, he suddenly expressed his hesitancy about my sister being a donor. When Oni informed me of this, it was as if the skies had fallen on me. I was dumbfounded; my heart shattered into pieces.

175

Not again!

I didn't know how the expression on my face might have looked at that time because immediately my sister said, "Don't worry. You will have your transplant. I am sure I can convince my husband and change his mind again."

We were supposed to be admitted on Sunday, but my sister had asked the hospital to allow her to come in on Monday so that she might have time to "talk things over" with her husband.

When my father heard about this change of date, he immediately ordered all his children home on Saturday so we could all get together in a family gathering to pray for the success of the upcoming operation. God bless his soul; he was the driving force that kept us siblings together. And even with short notice, we had a good time gathering and praying and listening to Abah's advice and counsel. I was deeply moved by this gesture of his. I am sure Oni was too. Arrangements were made for Oni's three daughters to be looked after by one of our sisters.

On Sunday afternoon when I was admitted, everything was in a bit of a rush. I got myself admitted alone first; Oni would come on Monday. I was a bit concerned, wondering if my brother-in-law would be unwavering in his reluctance to allow my sister to go through the operation just yet. But Oni was confident she could pacify him, so all that was left for me to do was pray that she was right.

The one thing I remember was the visit by the anaesthetist who would be handling the anaesthesia during the operation. A pleasant-looking young man, he asked a few questions. And then after that some blood was taken, and I was told it was to test for my clotting factor—the PT and the APTT2. As the blood was drawn from me, suddenly I was reminded of the time when I needed blood transfusion.

I had been highly anaemic at that time, and so a blood transfusion was ordered. Prior to administering the blood, a sample of my blood was taken to determine my blood group and not too long after that a bag of A+ blood was pumped slowly into the vein in my arm.

At first, I did not feel anything out of the ordinary. I had undergone blood transfusion previously, and apart from the discomfort of having to stay immobile for some time, it was not anything to be wary of. However, on this occasion, what started out as an ordinary blood transfusion turned out to be quite a nightmare. It started out with me suddenly feeling uncomfortably warm. That slowly escalated to an uncontrollable itch, with red spots breaking out all over my arm. Then came the big bonus—the itch spread to my face, and I started scratching.

Almost immediately, I felt a sudden thickening on my face. My eyes got progressively more difficult to open, and still the itching persisted. Not being able to see what was happening to my face, I asked the patient on the next bed if I looked all right. The shocked horror on her face almost made me jump from my bed. I grew extremely anxious and agitated.

Luck has it that, at that precise moment, the on-call doctor came around to attend to one of the patients in the rather crowded second-class ward. (At that time, getting into the first class was still almost impossible; apparently, they seemed to be always full.)

As soon as I spotted the doctor, I immediately called him and asked for his attention. As he turned around to look at me, I could see his face slowly change from shocked surprise to a quirky smile that he could not quite control, and later, he burst into audible laughter. That riled me up a bit. There I was feeling anxious and worried, and the doctor had the gall to laugh at me! He came up to me and immediately could make a diagnosis. Looking at the tube from my arm attached to the bag of transfusion, I noticed him making an effort to curb his smile before he finally spoke out.

"Allergic reaction," he exclaimed simply.

I looked up at the bag; it was boldly labelled, "A positive".

I tried to speak up, but with difficulty, as my cheeks were so swollen, they pressed tightly on my lips. "But I have type A+ blood, doctor," I protested.

He looked at me for a moment, looking as if he was measuring me up. "Even so, occasionally patients do get allergic reactions," he replied.

That caught my curiosity. "So, what may have caused the allergy?" I queried, momentarily forgetting my condition.

The doctor just shrugged, and that was that. I just had to accept the brush-off.

He said something to the nurse (who was smiling as well, looking at my face), and then she came over and stopped the blood transfusion. She pulled out the needle from inside me and pressed a cotton pad over it until the blood stopped. Free at last, I rushed to the toilet to look at my face.

My face had indeed bloated to twice the size, making my eyes and lips just mere slits on my face. My nose had swelled up so that I could hardly see its not-so-high bridge on my face. I was horrified, but at the same time, I couldn't stop the laughter that was bubbling from inside me. It was no wonder both the doctor and nurse found it hilarious looking at me.

When I returned to my bed, the nurse was waiting for me with a syringe and cotton pad in a small trough. I was given an injection to reduce the swelling. After some time, I could feel the swelling getting smaller, and the itching soon stopped. It turned out that, every once in a while, even after the blood had been screened, the patient may get an allergic reaction. All this happened prior to my contracting TB, so I was always left wondering if I had caught the tuberculosis bacteria from that particular blood transfusion.

I was relieved to see my sister Oni's face appear in the doorway of the second-class ward the day before the operation. Her bed was already reserved next to mine. Seeing her cheerful smiling face, I was relieved and convinced that she had managed to pacify her husband that all would be well and that there was nothing to worry about.

I could not have been more wrong! I found out much later that my brother-in-law had lost his cool. The truth was that, from the very beginning, my brother-in-law was a bit worried about the idea of my sister being a donor. I learnt much later through one of their daughters, that probably my brother-in-law feared something going wrong, as his three children were still young at that time—the youngest being only 5. Over time, I gathered he put the worry to the back of his mind. But I reckoned that, with the sudden announcement of the date of surgery being brought forward and with hardly a week's time to prepare for the event, his anxiety clouded his rational thoughts.

Torn between giving his full consent yet at the same time fearful for what could go wrong, he resorted to an angry silent protest. Apparently, he left the house and did not return home the following afternoon. He had made it clear he was not sending my sister off to hospital that Monday morning. I can only guess that he had probably gone off to his "silent cave" to think things over and learn to finally accept that his wife was set on her decision.

I don't blame my brother-in-law at all. His fears and anxiety were real and valid. Any major surgery has its own risks. He had three young daughters to think of after all. It was a heavy burden he had to shoulder. He must surely be thinking that my sister didn't need to do this. Yet, on the other hand, he had seen how renal failure had affected his own sister and how Oni had taken care of her. Perhaps his conscience told him he should consent to his wife being my donor. I know it was a difficult position I had placed him in.

God bless my sister Oni. I can only begin to wonder the strength she had to muster to persevere with her decision to donate her kidney to me and especially to put up a cheerful front in front of me. On that Monday morning, what had happened was, in the absence of her husband, she had to leave her daughters with the neighbours, trusting them to take care of the girls until her husband returned. She then packed her clothes and boarded a bus to the hospital to be admitted—all by herself. She must surely have felt so alone and abandoned; anyone would. And what could possibly have passed through her mind when she said goodbye to her children?

Yet, above all, when she arrived at the hospital ward, she came up to me and said that all things had been taken care of, and we were good to go for the transplant. It is obvious today why she acted the way she did—she did not want me to feel worried or guilty or awkward about the situation between her and her husband. I knew she was concerned about my mental state; she was putting my welfare ahead of hers. How can you even remotely repay someone as thoughtful and generous of heart as that? Someone who would put the welfare of others before herself? Truly I am humbled—and even more after I discovered this truth as told by my niece. I know that to this very day, my sister would never have spoken once about the dispute she'd had with her husband the day before the operation if I had not queried her personally.

As I reflect now, I guess if I had any say, I would suggest that any donors and their loved ones be given the outlet to discuss things with a counsellor if so required or necessary. All parties involved should be allowed to speak their minds or qualms, and all need to understand what the surgery involves and the risks. Inevitably, for a donor who has a family, as in the case of my sister Oni, all of the family members are affected after all.

In my blissful ignorance, I was beside myself with joy to have my beloved sister assigned to the bed beside me. I told her about the previous anaesthetist visit. And no sooner had I done that than another anaesthetist came to talk to my sister. I remember her specifically advising the doctor of her asthmatic condition and of her very sensitive nose. The anaesthetist noted all.

Later in the evening, my husband came to visit, and Oni remembered well he brought two *kuih pau* (steamed buns filled with various fillings) for us—one each. Oni recalled she relished it as if it was the last cake she would have.

A little while later, Oni's husband dropped by. Once again, to me at that time, he seemed composed and calm. I had no knowledge of the dispute they had had the day before. He even went as far as to wish the both of us well.

"I give my permission for your sister to donate her kidney to you. I wish both of you well and may God be with you both," he said sombrely.

I was humbled. "Thank you for letting my sister donate her kidney. God willing, everything will be all right," I replied, trying my best to reassure him.

When visiting hours were over, a nurse came and called me to the treatment room. I learnt from the nurse that I needed my bowel to be absolutely empty of contents in preparation for the surgery. It was not a very modest procedure when she pumped the cold fluid into me. But even in my embarrassment, curiosity got the better of me, and I managed to ask the nurse what she was giving me. Smilingly, she simply replied "soap solution". And I believed her. This was what I had been led to believe all this while. It was only in the process of writing of this book that I found out through a doctor-student of mine that it was definitely *not* soap water but a chemical solution that induced bowel movement.

And it darn did the work of soap water for all I cared. My bowel was in havoc—churning and squeezing; it was all I could do to rush to the toilet and kick the door shut in the nick of time before I exploded. My gut felt like it was being pulled down as well; there was just no stopping it. I cannot recall how long I stayed in the toilet, but when I finally returned to my bed, I was as exhausted as a soldier back from the battlefield. To my (devilish) delicious pleasure, another patient informed me, as I was looking around for my sister, that Oni too was ushered to the treatment room by the nurse. I knew immediately that she was about to face the same fate as I had.

To my surprise, however, a few minutes passed before Oni walked back steadily to the ward. Her face looked dazed and disoriented, and I knew why. She had been subjected to the same embarrassing treatment and could not quite get over her shock.

"Well, what happened?" I asked expectantly.

She smiled nervously and told me what had happened. Then she added, "I think they want me to empty my bowel."

She thinks?

What? Couldn't she know already? And hadn't she already gone?

"So … haven't you been yet?" I asked, genuinely shocked.

Oni just shook her head. I could not believe this; half suspecting that the nurse had not given enough volume of the purging solution.

"Oh, come on! I went running off to the toilet like my life depended on it, and you don't feel anything?" I cried aloud.

And then it happened. Just as she was about to reply, her face suddenly contorted with agony. A deathly growl escaped her lips and she said hoarsely, "Oooooh … I need to go, oooh!" and she was out of the room in no time.

Watching her in pain probably induced my still as yet unrecovered bowel and I felt the urge again. Immediately jumping out of bed, I raced her to the toilet. By the time we got there, we were both laughing and crying out in urgency simultaneously. To make matters worse, the toilets were fully occupied, except for two. That would have been fine, if one of them was not soiled with a used, unflushed toilet bowl. For the love of God Almighty! Both of us made a dash for the cleaner toilet, but because I had gone through the worst, whilst Oni was just about to start her torturous ordeal, I was no match for her, and I won the better seat. I laughed my head off when Oni jumped onto the used toilet bowl, kicking the door shut with a loud bang and wailed, "Ooooh … I don't care, dirty or not, I need to go!" My loud giggles were drowned by the "expletives" from the bottom end of her digestive tract.

Both of us were spent by the time we returned to the ward. I still could not help laughing, as I was well on my way to recovery. But not Oni; she was still feeling the contractions and was pressing on to her abdomen. She was indeed in a desperate state. I was just enjoying myself too much watching her discomfort and laughing at her pained expression.

Just as the laughter was waning off, out of nowhere, a young naval officer, looking dashingly handsome in his full white uniform, appeared before us. Our beds were the nearest to the entrance of the ward, so we were the first he spoke to.

"Excuse me, but could either of you be Lili's sister from Klang? I am her friend," he said clearly and politely. "Lili said that I could find both her sisters here in the second class wing of Ward 4A," he continued.

"Yes, yes we are Lili's sisters," I stammered on behalf of Oni, who was still trying to contain her pain. I was so not used to having strangers visit me.

The young naval officer explained that he was a friend of our youngest sister, Lili, and since he was around in Kuala

Lumpur on a certain assignment, he had decided to come visit us and wish us luck. He then turned to my sister Oni and said gently, "Are you the one who is going to have the transplant?"

I nearly burst into laughter when it dawned on me why he had assumed Oni to be the sick one. She certainly looked ill enough with all the recent purging and, as of the moment, still suppressing the urge.

"Oh no," my sister replied sheepishly. I guess she had realised too why the officer had mistaken her for me, the sick one.

I could not really tell what the gentleman felt at his mistake, for he masked his expression well. *A true officer to the bone*, I thought. He made some light talk with us, concentrating more on my sister when he learnt that Oni was the older between the two of us. I was happy with that, always preferring to be the observer.

The officer was immaculately dressed in his white uniform, he stood as stiff as a rod whilst talking, and his attempts at smiling were just the faintest quirks at the sides of his lips. I wondered how Lili knew him, but he was good-looking enough, and I guessed his uniform must have been what attracted Lili to befriend him. Lili always seemed to be attracted to men in uniform. His visit was brief.

When he finally left, once again, we continued our laughter—well, me laughing at Oni mostly.

Later in the night, we were both surprised by a visit from our big brother Aral. Since visiting hours were over, we had to sneak out of the ward to speak with him. We talked and laughed with him as Oni regaled Aral with the purging incident. But we later sobered up momentarily when a hospital attendant passed by us pushing a trolley with a body covered up to the face. We knew immediately that a patient had just passed away and was being taken off to the mortuary.

The silence was only momentary though. Big brother Aral who was always wary of hospitals immediately exclaimed, "That's scary. I'd better go home soon."

My dear big brother Aral—one can totally count on him in so many other things, rain or shine. He cared for me once when I was pregnant. He had taken me along with his pregnant wife for check-up. On the way back, I vomited all over the back seat of his car. Without so much as the slightest complain, Aral patiently scrubbed the seat clean. But pain was something he was not too keen to bear for the sake of others. He has always been honest and open with whatever he felt in his heart, and that was what I have always respected in him.

When Aral finally left, I was still feeling fresh and somewhat excited. I could see Oni was not tired either. I guess we were both restless and anxious for the next day to come. We were walking around and trying to sneak back to our beds unnoticed. Little did we realise that the medical officer on call did notice us. As soon as we got to our beds, a nurse promptly turned up and handed us a tablet each.

"To help you get a good night's sleep," she said.

Recalling the night, according to Oni, I went off soon after, sleeping like a log, oblivious to the world. For Oni, on the other hand, the tablet did not do much to relax her, and she finally fell asleep much, much later. It was probably because of my condition that I got knocked off quickly and easily. Oni told me later how she envied the way I could fall asleep so quickly and so peacefully.

CHAPTER

15

—

A New Beginning

When God pushes you to the edge of difficulty,
trust Him fully, because two things can happen;
either He'll catch you when you fall, or
He will teach you how to fly.

19 July 1988

The day had finally arrived. I woke up early, took my bath, and spent a good length of time praying to God for a successful operation.

"Oh, Allah, whatever is about to happen today, let me continue to be faithful to You. But more importantly, may You be pleased with me. Oh, Allah, I beg your forgiveness for all my sins—either intentionally or unintentionally committed. Above all, Oh, Allah, I pray for my sister Oni's safety more than I pray for mine. Please, please make her come out fine after the operation, regardless of what the outcome will be for me. Oh, Allah, if this is to be my last day, then I pray that You ease my affairs at the moment of death and ease my affairs after death and grant me a place in Heaven. Our Lord! Cause not our hearts to stray after You have guided us and bestow upon us mercy from Your Presence. You, only You, art the Bestower. Amen."

Oni was up and about too, getting herself prepared. We were both made to wear the hospital gowns. And since we were already on the "none orally" since the night before, there was not much else to do but wait to be taken to the operating rooms. Between the two of us, there was no emotional small talk. It was as if we were both prepping ourselves up for the event, and we were ready to go.

It was not a long wait actually. Just barely after seven in the morning, two trolleys appeared before us to wheel us to the operating rooms. The nurses covered our hair up in the hospital with white scarves before giving both of us an injection—presumably to keep us calm.

Strangely, as far as I can recall, I was feeling calm—something that I would describe as quiet acceptance of whatever was about to happen. Just before we were wheeled off, I remember shaking hands and hugging my sister Oni tightly. It was hard to let go. I tried to convey my utmost feelings of gratitude and love in that hug. I was bereft of speech; no words seemed appropriate enough to convey the great love and gratitude I felt at that moment. This was it—our defining moments as siblings. Still, I no longer felt that rush of adrenaline. I was feeling quite calm. Oni looked like she was too. Perhaps whatever was in the injection was beginning to have its effects on our systems.

As we were wheeled out of the ward, to my greatest delight, I saw my husband waiting to see me off. And not too far from him, I saw my older sister Kak Mah and two of Oni's daughters were with her too—Inaz who was ten at that time, and her younger sister, Olin, who was only five. They had spent the night at Kak Mah's house, and she had brought them to send off their mother before the operation. Oni's oldest daughter, Emma, who was twelve at that time, could not come along, as she had her primary national exam on that very same day. We were told she would be coming in the evening with her father.

Although Oni could only see her two daughters just briefly, I am sure it made her feel comforted to know that her children would be waiting for her after the surgery. I was relieved and happy for her.

As for my husband, we just held hands for a short while. Like Aral, my husband had always been wary of hospitals—blood, trolleys, and patients made him anxious. But as we held hands, I knew he was wishing me well and praying for my safety.

We were led through narrow corridors, which I was not so familiar with. Oni followed behind on her trolley. Soon we arrived at the operating waiting room, where I felt terribly cold. Oni's trolley was parked next to mine, but only briefly before she was led off first into one of the rooms. Soon after that, I was taken to another room. That was the last I saw of my sister Oni before the operation.

What ensued after that is quite a blur to me now. But one thing was for sure—I was feeling calm and peaceful. As the doctors and nurses got busy on me, one of the nurses started to make small talk with me.

"What's your name, dear?"

I stated my name clearly.

"You are in here today to have your renal transplant done, right?"

I could only nod. When she said it in that way, it felt like the truth had finally caught up with me. Still lying down, I was then deftly transferred to the operating table, where I remember staring at big round bright lights looking down on me. But I was getting sleepy as tubes were expertly attached to my body.

Then one of the staff spoke to me, "Your sister is in the next room; they have started the procedure with her already."

My heart missed a beat to hear that news. I nodded again, making a special prayer in my heart that all would go well with her.

I knew my turn was about to start when one of the nurses came up close to me and said, "Before we start, why don't you say the *Shahadah* first?" she suggested gently.

The Shahadah is the declaration of the Islamic faith professed by every Muslim. We have been taught that no one should die without announcing the Shahadah. So, I did. God forbid, but in case things did not go as hoped, if anything were to happen to me, then I would certainly want to die as a Muslim and to meet my Creator as a Muslim and live the eternal life in the hereafter as a Muslim. Nothing else would matter.

My internal prayers were interrupted when a male voice addressed me gently.

"Now, Norhafizah, I want you to try and count backwards from ten to one. Can you do that for me?"

Here we go.

"Ten, nine, eight, seven ..." I cannot recall anymore after that.

I woke up feeling very cold and confused. Somebody was slowly waking me up from my deep sleep. Was I asleep? Wasn't I scheduled for my transplant? Hadn't they started yet on me?

The last thing I remembered was the nurse mentioning that they had started on Oni.

Oni! How was she doing?

"My sister ... how is she?" I cried out. But my voice was just a mere whisper. Why was I feeling so weak and sleepy?

A gentle voice spoke to me. "Your sister is fine; she is being sent to the ward even as we speak. The operation is over, Fizah. Everything went well. You are going to be all right now."

The operation was over? I couldn't quite grasp what that meant. I was feeling too sleepy to really appreciate what was happening. But I do remember saying, "Alhamdulillah" (All praise be to Allah), mainly for my sister.

I lost track of my whereabouts again.

"Fizah, look who is out there at the window." A nurse's gentle voice once again woke me up from my stupor.

I was feeling weak. I could hardly open my eyes. But I realised I was no longer in the cold operating theatre. I was on a bed in the middle of a small room. Looking ahead, I could see, through the glass pane on the wall, other small rooms ahead.

The window to the outside was on my left, and I tried my best to focus on the shadowy figures waving at me from the other side of the glass windowpane. I finally made out my father in his wheelchair and a few of my siblings. I could not quite make out the rest, but I was pretty sure I saw my husband's smiling face too. I tried to smile and wave at them. But I was just feeling too drowsy and confused.

Later, my family said I had looked as pale as a ghost and looked so small. And they told me that, as usual, my father cried to see me like that. I guess everyone would look like that after a major operation—that look of vulnerability. I was also informed later that, from the moment I was wheeled off to the operating room, my family only saw me back in the ICU at 6.30 in the evening. I had lost any conscious recollection of myself for about ten hours.

I was only more aware of my surroundings later in the night, when I started to feel slightly uncomfortable. I noticed the nurses going in and out of my room quite frequently, monitoring my condition. One of them asked if I was feeling any pain. And when I replied that I was feeling a bit uncomfortable, she informed me that she would give me some painkiller soon, which would, naturally, make me sleepy again. I was told I would be in this supine position for the next twenty-four hours, after which I would need to ambulate myself. I peeped below and saw the catheter coming out of me. To my great delight, the urine bag was steadily filling up. I was passing out a good volume of urine. I reckoned the nurse saw me looking at the urine bag and anticipated my apprehension.

She smiled gently, and I remember her patting me on the shoulder. "Your condition looks promising. All praise be to God."

Yes, all praise be to God.

I fell asleep again.

Friday, three days post-transplant

The catheter had been taken out, and the doctors were pleased with my progress thus far. I was fairly mobile and no longer in much pain. Things did look promising. I remember feeling very optimistic and, if I may say so, my twenty-plus young self again. But I must say, the best part was that I was passing normal amounts of urine. To many people, passing urine would be so mundane that I have even seen some people getting annoyed when they feel the urge to pee at the wrong time, especially when they are absorbed in doing whatever they are doing. For me, just to sit on the bowl and feel the rush as I relieved my bladder was exciting and humbling at the same time.

After a long while, I finally felt alive once again. And to realise that, together with the urine, the toxic wastes from my body were being removed left me with the feeling of being vibrantly healthy. That feeling of vitality was just awesome. I was simply on top of the world.

But the blessing was not to end there just yet. That Friday morning, when I went to the toilet, to my greatest delight, I discovered that I was having my menses. I was sure it was no coincidence, as Oni was having her menses when the transplant was performed. For the past two years, I'd only had my menstruation twice a year. And then, in 1988, the menses had totally stopped. I think perhaps it had something to do with my being severely anaemic following my haemodialysis. I was just so thrilled I could have shouted. It was a blessing for two reasons.

Firstly, it meant that my body was beginning to function normally again. Secondly, it meant I was relieved from my duties of performing my daily prayers. Initially, I was not feeling too comfortable having to pray with the catheter and urine bag still attached to me. Still, the five daily prayers are the first prerequisite to identifying ourselves as Muslims. Prayer is remembrance of God. And I, of all people, felt especially compelled to remember God after all that I had been through and to be given this second chance at life.

So, when I found out that I was having my menstruation that Friday morning and thus excused from the obligatory duty of performing my five daily prayers, I felt it was like a double blessing from God. Not only was I reprieved from my duties under that compromised situation, but to me personally, to have my period come back only three days after transplant was like a signal from my body that I was on my way to recovery, that my body was accepting the kidney donated by my sister, and that all my systems were back on the go.

I was suddenly acutely aware of the question asked by God again and again in the chapter Ar Rahman from the Holy Quran:

> Which is it, of the favours of your Lord, that ye deny? Lord of the two Easts, and Lord of the two Wests! Which is it, of the favours of your Lord, that ye deny? (The Lord of Mercy [Ar Rahman] 55:16–18)

Meanwhile, I learnt that, after the transplant, Oni was sent to the general ward in the afternoon, where she stayed for four days before she was discharged. She was healing very well. My husband had come to visit her and then took her home to reunite with her family.

I was into my second week in the ICU when, one evening, an Indian boy was admitted into the ICU and placed in the first cubicle. Although I was in the last cubicle, the glass pane on the wall in every cubicle enabled me to see what was happening in other cubicles as well. It turned out that the young Indian boy had been involved in a motorcycle accident and had injured his kidneys quite severely. When one of the nurses came in to check on me, my curiosity got the better of me and I wanted to know what had happened. As the nurse recounted what had happened to the poor boy, I felt very sorry for his bad luck. At the same time, I could not help smiling at the unfortunate situation he had gotten into in the first place.

Apparently, he had been the pillion rider on his friend's motorcycle. Both were wearing helmets at the time of the accident, but alas, the rider only just had his on; he had not tied it securely on his head. As they were coasting the roadside on the motorcycle, they happened to chance upon a young girl walking by the road.

"So, as you can expect when boys see pretty girls, their heads will turn. Now here comes the sad but quite funny part, Fizah," the nurse carried on. "As soon as the rider turned back his head towards the road, only his head turned, his helmet did not follow because he had not tied his helmet securely. Can you imagine that? So, all he could see was the dark on the inside of his helmet before he ran into a lamp post and sent his poor friend flying off onto the road."

My jaw dropped in disbelief as I listened to the story. It was an accident that could have been so easily avoided had the motorcyclist just taken the extra trouble to fasten his helmet securely. It was such an unfortunate accident indeed. The rider was killed almost instantly, and the pillion rider was in critical condition. I learnt that he had seriously injured his kidneys, which explained why he was in the same ICU unit as I was.

I guess looking at the serious condition the poor boy was in, with all the strange tubes attached to his body, and watching other patients come and go from the other ICU cubicles took its toll on me. I grew anxious, and as a result, my blood pressure was slightly raised. When the doctor came to make his rounds and noticed this, I jokingly argued, "I think it's from watching the critical state that all those guys in the other cubicles are in, doctor. The longer I stay here, I think my blood pressure will continue to rise."

To my surprise, the doctor agreed with me. He declared I was now fit to go home. It was common for renal transplant patients to be placed in the general ward after a bout in the ICU before being fully discharged. In my case, however, the doctor was satisfied that I was fit enough to be sent home straight. I was exhilarated.

So, it was decided that I would be discharged the following day, on a Saturday. I was supplied with a full load of medication—prednisolone, Imuran, B6 vitamins, and also a supply of isoniazid and rifampicin to prevent recurrence of my tuberculosis. To this day, I am still on these medications (my prednisolone medication has been reduced to a minimum dose over time). And I'll continue to be on these medications for the rest of my life.

I had been in the ICU for twelve days, constantly under the keen eyes of the nurses in the ward. They were as friendly as they were serious with their job. And they were experts at what they did—caring for post-transplant patients like me. I was well taken care of, and now I was about to leave the care of those nurses and be on my own for the first time, post-transplant. Suddenly, I was filled with anxiety. In the ICU, I had nurses specialised in their field taking care of me around the clock. What if anything were to go wrong when I was at home? There had been one instance when I was in ICU that I had some pain passing urine, and the nurses were quick to respond. Another thing that worried me was that, in the ICU, I was in an almost sterile condition, and I was alone in my cubicle almost all the time. When I got home, I would be exposed to the world out there. I was really beginning to feel anxious.

Yet at the same time, I could not wait to go home and continue where I left off with my life. A new lease on life was awaiting me out there. It was really a moment of dilemma for me—between fear and hope.

Before I was allowed to go home, the bandage over my graft site was removed, showing a scar about fifteen centimetres long, with twelve stitches on it running in a curve on my left abdomen. The nurse then sprayed a fine film of protective covering over the scar. I was feeling good; there was no pain there. I had three months of medical leave, and throughout those times, I must avoid going out to crowded places as much as possible.

The doctor instructed that, if I should go out, I must make sure to wear a face mask at all times. The first three months are the most critical to a renal transplant patient. Extra care must be taken to make sure we do not get any infections. For the first three months, I had to come to the hospital for check-up every week, on Wednesdays. I was told to avoid as much as possible eating outside food, and it was preferable if I stayed away from salty foods. I was determined to obey the doctor's instructions to the letter. I wanted to be well again!

What I did not anticipate at all was that my first trial upon returning home would be the journey home itself. Over the years that I'd suffered my renal failure, my urine output had grown progressively scanty, and I was urinating less and less frequently. My bladder was hardly ever full. However, almost immediately after the transplant, my urine output returned to normal, and my bladder began filling up quite frequently; on top of that, we transplant patients are encouraged to drink more. In the ICU, I was always reminded not to hold back from passing urine. In fact, I was not able to contain myself. My bladder, for many years, had not been used to holding in a large volume of urine. As a result, in the beginning just after the transplant, I was constantly going to the toilet since my bladder was still sensitive to the stretch.

It was about an hour's drive from the hospital to my home— provided there was no heavy traffic. Unfortunately, on that Saturday afternoon, traffic was heavy, and our car was moving slowly. About halfway through the highway, I was growing desperately in need of a toilet.

"Oh my God, I need to pee. My abdomen is beginning to hurt," I cried out to my husband. "Can't you go any faster? I can't contain it much longer." I was growing desperate.

"We can stop at a public toilet or at the petrol station if you want," my husband suggested. I remember the worried look on his face.

"No, I am not taking any risk of infection right now," I protested. "Just please hurry."

I was determined to hold it in. At one point I must have looked silly sitting beside my husband squirming and writhing in desperation. I started to laugh at the hilarity of my situation and cry at the same time from the pain of urgency. For the first time, after such a long while, my body was perspiring from the heat and the stress to contain my bladder. I watched in amazement as the pores on my arms glistened with sweat. I had not sweated in a long, long time. It made me feel so terribly healthy I could sing with jubilant joy. That was certainly a moment to remember—all mixed emotions rolled into one. I'd never felt more alive!

As soon as I got home, the bathroom was the first place I headed to relieve myself. How befitting—a pleasantly potent reminder that I was well and normal again, that I now had a fully functioning kidney that would fill my bladder with urine from time to time. I had beaten the odds—for now. I had survived ESRD. It wasn't quite the end for me just yet.

A new lease on life was waiting in front of me.

Thank you, God—all praise be to Him.

For the first three months after my renal transplant, it was mainly to and fro for my medical appointments every week and wearing my mask every time I went out. Most of the time, I stayed indoors. But as the three-month confinement neared its end, I had some serious shopping to do.

Within the three months, my weight had risen from forty kilograms to seventy kilograms!

Thanks to the steroids. I was on a maximum dose of 12 tablets per day, which really boosted my appetite. Where people take two slices of bread for breakfast, I could easily finish a loaf of the raisin bread. My appetite was always good. And I always made sure I drank the whole eight litres of plain water every single day. It was no wonder I gained tremendous weight within the three months.

That wasn't the only thing with the steroids.

My mood swings were something I found very difficult to adjust to in the beginning. One moment, I was laughing away; the very next, I could be just as agitated. It required a great effort for me to control those mood swings, given that my husband had to bear the brunt of those unfortunate incidences when I would just be in a foul mood for no apparent reason. I mentioned this to the doctor on one of my visits. As a reply, he pushed towards me a thick hard-covered book.

"Here, this book lists all the side effects of steroids."

Oh my! I stared at the book, jaw gaping. I didn't even dare touch the book to see what was inside. The sheer thickness of the book said enough. I realised that, since I would be on steroids for the rest of my life, or for as long as the kidney served me, the side effects would be inevitable. It would be up to me to manage it. I told myself I could overcome them, God willing.

Thank God Almighty, all those side effects were only temporary, and they are all behind me now (even though the long-term side effects of those years of taking steroids are more prominently felt now).

The first thing I did after my three-month transplant confinement was over was take that long overdue honeymoon with my husband. We went up to Fraser's Hill, a highland resort destination nestled among the mountains of Pahang and about a two-hour drive from Kuala Lumpur. The cooling climate, reminiscent of mild British weather, was a good escape for my husband and me from the city. It was something to remember. It was the beginning of life for me once again.

EPILOGUE

Never regret.
If it's good, it's wonderful.
If it's bad, it's experience.
—Victoria Holt

It is now more than thirty-two years since my renal transplant way back in 1988. Many things have happened since.

The first thing that must be mentioned is that I found out that the more recent patients no longer go through the intermittent peritoneal dialysis procedure. Good for them. Presumably, this is because haemodialysis is made readily available today, either in government sectors or in private hospitals and health care agencies. This is wonderful to know; as I have always insisted, I wouldn't want anyone to have to experience IPD, not even my worst enemy. Also, under certain circumstances, a kidney patient today may be allowed to carry through her pregnancy under close monitoring by the hospital.

There are several alternatives to peritoneal dialysis today, apart from haemodialysis. There is still the CAPD of course, which gives the patient a world of freedom. There is now the APD (automated peritoneal dialysis). In APD, just as in other peritoneal dialysis, a catheter is inserted into the peritoneal cavity for the inflow and outflow of the dialysis solution. In APD, however, an APD machine controls all three phases of dialysis cycles—draining off the used solution, refilling with fresh solution, and monitoring the dwell time (the time the solution remains in the peritoneal cavity). The machine does the dialysis ten hours a night while the patient sleeps. And once disconnected from the machine in the morning, the patient is free to go about his or her daily activities as usual. The prognosis for renal failure patients on dialysis now looks more promising.

Post-transplant

I lost another child through a miscarriage in 1990. After that, I was under the care of O&G to try to conceive, but things were not that easy. My mother (who passed away in 2011, may God bless her soul and place her among the pious), used to lament, "If only you can get one child; that will be good enough for you and your husband."

Abah had a slightly different view. "Don't say it that way. Instead say, 'May you have one child first.' God is All powerful. Nothing is impossible with God," he would correct her.

"You will have your child when I am gone," my father told me once.

I believed him.

His prayers came true.

Sadly, Abah never got to see my son. He passed away on 27 November 1991(may God bless his soul and place him among the pious). True enough, exactly nine months later, at midnight of 28 August 1992, I gave birth to a beautiful baby boy, my son Ahmad Ashraf Ilman, via a caesarean section.

I was hospitalised for two whole months prior to delivery. All those days in hospital were worth it. Due to steroid effects, I developed chronic sebaceous hyperplasia that altered my face badly during my pregnancy. I must admit I might have even looked like a hideous monster. I was glad to spend my pregnancy days in the one-room hospital ward. (Thankfully, the blatant swelling of my face reduced immediately after birth.) It was all the best for everyone that I was hospitalised and did not have to face the public. Plus, I had the best gynaecologist I could possibly hope for, who took care of me throughout my pregnancy.

My nephrologist had said that I was allowed only this one child, given that I'd already had a previous pregnancy two years earlier, even though it had ended in miscarriage.

Dr Marlik, my gynaecologist, had something different to say though. "You are still young and strong. I am confident it's okay for you to have another child, as long as it's before you're 35. So, I'm not going to do the tubal ligation for you just yet," he advised.

There was certainly no arguing from me. I was 31 at that time, and if there was any chance to have another child, I would definitely take it. In 1994, I performed the Umrah (lesser haj) for the first time in my life. And in front of the Holy Kaaba, I prayed for another child. At that point in time, my menstruation had slowed down to only once every three months—significantly lowering my chances to be pregnant again.

My prayers were answered yet again.

All praise be to God, in February 1996, I was utterly shocked to discover that I was once again pregnant. Initially when I reported my pregnancy to the nephrology department, the doctors were not too happy. This time, they warned me that the next pregnancy would definitely be terminated. Thankfully, they allowed me this one last time.

My little boy, Ahmad Zakiy Mohsin, was born through normal delivery at 11 p.m. on 11 November 1996—just three days before my thirty-fifth birthday. I specifically wanted him to be named after Dato Dr Zaki Morad, who was a significant figure throughout my ESRD days.

I am most grateful to Allah Almighty for His never-ending blessings upon me. Both my boys never got to taste even a single drop of mother's milk. I was not allowed to breastfeed simply because of the many medication I was on. It is said that children who are not breastfed are not as whole and balanced as those who are breastfed. But I know God understands my condition. Since I could never breastfeed them, I made doubly sure they never lacked anything else—especially the security and love every child deserves.

My boys have done well in their studies. Ashraf is now a doctor himself. And his younger brother, Zakiy, has graduated with a degree in psychology and is currently employed in one of the biggest companies in Malaysia. I am ever more thankful to God that both of them are good obedient young men today—to both God and their parents. They are both aware of what their mother had gone through to be where she is today. And only God knows how much I love the both of them.

Ashraf is married and his wife, Adzkia, has gifted me my beloved grandchildren, Aya Camila and Yahya, aged five and two respectively at the time of this writing. When Aya was born, I could not talk about her without tears in my eyes—tears of utter gratefulness and gratitude to God for letting me live long enough to see and get to know my grandchildren. The feelings of gratitude just overwhelm me to this very day.

Zakiy too has also recently married. He and his wife, Nur Nasreen, were married last December amid the Covid-19 pandemic that remains prevalent as of this writing.

Other, more personal dreams have been realised too over the years. Taking full advantage of my new lease on life, I proceeded to further my studies in the fields I'd always been interested in—educational, psychology, and counselling. My teaching profession has become my passion; I enjoyed my students just as much as I enjoyed teaching itself. I taught biology and science for the most part of my career. Many of my students have left school, but they still maintain close contact with me. It gives me great pleasure, which is difficult to describe, to have students come up to me and tell me that they understood my lessons and enjoyed my classes.

However, in later years, the effects of prolonged medication, especially the steroids, took its toll on me. For that reason, I took an optional retirement in 2014 at the age of 53. The retirement age in Malaysia is 60.

In my effort to minimise the side effects of the steroids, I eventually developed an interest in alternative medicine, especially in colour vibration therapy and aromatherapy. This later led to a medical degree in alternative medicine. I am so thankful to God that practicing alternative medicine has helped me a lot over the years, especially in dealing with the emotional aspects of being a transplant patient.

Being immunologically suppressed has its constant worries and being on steroids for so long has left me with a myriad of side effects. Due to the chronic sebaceous hyperplasia I developed on my face, sometimes I feel very self-conscious to have people stare at me. At times, it even takes a lot of effort to maintain my self-esteem. But I must thank God that what I went through during my ESRD days has given me enough mental and spiritual strength to stay above my problems.

And then in 2008, I achieved my lifelong dream. I finally got published with my first book, *After the Rain*, a novel for young teenagers. That was the most satisfying moment of my life. (To date, I have eight books to my name, all praise be to God.)

Still, as age catches up on me, and with the prolonged intake of steroids, I now have diabetes and hypertension. Recently, I have begun sleeping using a CPAP (continuous positive air pressure) machine for my obstructive sleep apnoea, which was duly diagnosed after I fell asleep at traffic lights—not once, but twice. Most recently, I now have spondylolisthesis, as well as spondylosis, not to mention osteoarthritis. This slowed down my teaching significantly and made me opt for an early retirement. But it was not before I was diagnosed with cirrhosis of the liver, following an infection of hepatitis C (which I probably contracted due to my steroid consumption). Thankfully, with the advent of new medication, I am today fully treated, and my liver is in the clear.

I accept them all; what does not kill me only makes me stronger. My body may not be as agile as others, but I know that I am living a wonderful life with my family—my husband, my two boys and their wives, and especially my beloved grandchildren. I have been blessed with wonderful moments of teaching and still keep in touch with many of my former students. My life is full and blessed.

And of my sister Oni

All three of Oni's daughters have graduated successfully and are married. She is now the proud grandmother of three handsome boys and three beautiful girls whom she takes pride in caring for. Along the way, Oni lost another organ—her gall bladder, when she was diagnosed with gall bladder stones.

She is still her jovial sunny self, still busy, and simply cannot sit around idly. So not long ago she took up her driving licence and now proudly drives her own car—scooting around with her grandchildren. Lately, she has taken up painting as a new hobby.

Oni and I still meet up whenever we can; she stays nearby to my house. She is 66 now.

Oni is very much the "second mother" to my boys. She gave up her job at a school canteen when my older son was born just so she could care for him when I was away at work. And that continued even until my second son was born. It was only when both of them started attending school that she no longer babysat them.

Personally, I don't know what I would have done without my beloved sister Oni. She certainly has made my post-transplant life smooth sailing, ever ready to lend a hand whenever I was in need of one. I am forever, till the end of my life, indebted to her. I could not find anyone better than her to take care of my boys. My sons simply adore her. I know that, if anything were to happen to me now, my boys would not be lacking in motherly love. My sister Oni, who my boys call Mak Mok, is just as important in my boys' lives as she is in mine.

Over the years, long after my transplant, I asked Oni again why she gave one of her kidneys to me. Her answer? "You are my sister. I love you."

As simple as that. I love her too—more than words can say.

I do not know how many years I have left in me. But the past thirty-two years have certainly been the best years of my life, despite the ups and downs of my health. Living on the fact that I was given a second chance in life has really taught me the meaning of appreciating every moment of my life and to be thankful to God Almighty for His mercy and blessings. I am very much aware that I was given this second chance in life, and I should not let that go in vain. My second chance must be for a reason. I know I have a purpose to fulfil. Now I no longer ask why I had ESRD; instead, I check frequently what God would want me to do in any particular situation at any particular time of my life.

Spiritually, I know, without a shadow of a doubt, that God is forever watching over me and that, for all my weaknesses, physically and spiritually, He is always near. Over the years, I have had my share of goof-ups too. I have, at times, in moments of heedlessness, bungled up my relationship with Him. I am not proud of those errors; I am remorseful. But every time, He would show me my erring ways and help get me back on track. I am hopeful of His promise:

> And Allah will not punish them, while they seek forgiveness. (Battle Gains [Al Anfal] 8:33)

Clearly, He hasn't given up on me, so I should not give up on His mercy or myself either. It is His love that has put me through this incredible episode in this journey of my life—giving me a better understanding of what life is all about and training me not to give up when things get rough. It's through this experience that He gave me that has shown to me the strength I have in me and has taught me to be more understanding and to empathise with the trials that afflict others. I have learnt not to be quick to judge, and I have learnt to be more open-minded—for each and every one of us has our own battles to contend with. If ever there is anything that I learnt, it's this: Never give up on God; good or bad though the outcome may appear, there is always something better that awaits us as long as we have faith in God.

Today, I embrace all possibilities. I know God is with me. I pray hard that my end will be as I hope for—the best of ends—as a Muslim, believing and placing my trust in the One God. If it is my time to go, and should death come to invite, I know I am only returning to Him after all.

Allah has been kind to me. No matter what trials I have been through, life has been good. My loved ones and close friends surround me in any moment of my life. With this second chance at life, I pray that I will become a humbler servant of Allah Almighty and that, in the hereafter, I will continue to receive His love and mercy. Above all, may He grant me the best of endings—His eternal paradise, the Jannah. I truly have a lot to be thankful for. And God says:

> If you are grateful, I will surely increase you (in favours). (Abraham [Ibrahim] 14:7)

Life is a possibility; death is a certainty. In the meantime, I continue to live to the best that I can.

Lightning Source UK Ltd.
Milton Keynes UK
UKHW041613240621
386092UK00001B/52